To

_____

From

_____

Date

_____

TOUCHED
by HEAVEN

More than a Coincidence...
True Stories of God's Miracles in Everyday Life

Guideposts

TOUCHED BY HEAVEN

ISBN: 978-0-8249-4521-3
ISBN: 0-8249-4521-2

Published by Guideposts
16 East 34th Street
New York, New York 10016
Guideposts.org

Distributed by Ideals Publications, a Guideposts company
2630 Elm Hill Pike, Suite 100
Nashville, TN 37214

Guideposts and *Ideals* are registered trademarks of Guideposts.

Acknowledgments
Every attempt has been made to credit the sources of copyrighted material used in this
book. If any such acknowledgment has been inadvertently omitted or miscredited,
receipt of such information would be appreciated.

Scripture references are from the following sources: The Holy Bible, King James
Version (KJV). The Holy Bible, New International Version®, NIV®. Copyright © 1973,
1978, 1984, 2011 by Biblica, Inc.™ Used by permission of Zondervan. All rights
reserved worldwide. The New King James Version (NKJV). Copyright © 1982 by
Thomas Nelson, Inc. Used by permission. The New American Standard Bible®
(NASB), Copyright © 1960, 1962, 1963, 1968, 1971, 1972, 1973, 1975, 1977, 1995 by
The Lockman Foundation. Used by permission.

Cover and interior design by Jeff Jansen | www.aestheticsoup.net
Cover photograph by Inmagine

Printed in China
10 9 8 7 6 5 4 3 2 1

CONTENTS

INTRODUCTION

Touched by Heaven is the first book in our new series based on the *Guideposts* column "Mysterious Ways." Drawing on fifty-plus years of publishing inspirational stories, we have collected some of its best-loved, uplifting stories, to reveal how faith works supernaturally in ordinary lives.

As you read these real-life encounters with God, you will find yourself looking more and more for His touch, His caring ways, His stepping into your own life. Often despite great odds, ordinary people discover a strength they never knew they had when they turn to God in difficult times. These stories introduce you to men and women who have a need but have no idea how it will be met. And then when they ask God for His guidance and care, He provides for them—often in ways beyond their wildest imagination.

May your faith be strengthened as you read these inspiring stories. And as you do, be prepared to shed any remaining doubt that God cares deeply for His children!

1
*I*NTERVENTION FROM *H*EAVEN

*I*f you say, "The LORD is my refuge," and you make the Most High your dwelling, no harm will overtake you, no disaster will come near your tent. For he will command his angels concerning you to guard you in all your ways; they will lift you up in their hands, so that you will not strike your foot against a stone.

PSALM 91:9–12 NIV

Lord, thank You for hearing us when we call to You for help!
You are a trustworthy Savior, and we put our hope in You.

In Need of a Friend

by Karen Kingsbury

———— ·〰· ————

Bonner Davis knew the end was near, but he could do nothing to change his situation. He had advanced throat cancer, mounting medical bills, and no way to pay for the experimental treatment that could save his life.

Bonner, a retired forest ranger, and his wife, Angela, lived in North Carolina where they existed on his meager pension and a faith bigger than the Smoky Mountains. Once in a while, Bonner would share his fears with Angela. She was his best friend, and though he looked forward to heaven, he didn't want to leave her.

Angela's answer was always the same. "God knows what we need, Bonner. I'm praying for a miracle and, somehow, somehow, I believe He'll give us one."

In nearby Spartanburg, millionaire Olsen Matthews was celebrating his sixtieth birthday. Single and without any close friends, Olsen chose to spend his day in the air. He was a novice pilot who always felt more complete when he was alone in his small Cessna plane.

Sunshine reigned that afternoon, and Olsen savored the familiar rush as he took to the air. He'd been in the air twenty minutes when the rush faded to a sort of soul-searching, which often happened when Olsen flew. What was life about, anyway? He had more money than he knew what to do with, but not a single person he could call a friend. Sure, Olsen had advisors and peers he did business with. But he had no family, no friend who cared about him.

This time as he flew, gazing down at the rolling hills and valleys, another thought filled Olsen's heart: What about God? All his life he'd denied the idea of both creation and Creator, but now, with his life waning toward the sunset years, he sometimes wondered.

What if God was real? What if he had a few things to do before he died in order to be right with that God? The possibility set his nerves on edge and made him wish once more for a friend, someone he could share his thoughts with. Perhaps even someone who knew something about God and why so many people believed in Him.

Olsen was about to turn his plane around and soar back over the mountains when he heard a sharp pop. At the same instant, the engine cut out. Olsen felt a wave of adrenaline rush through his veins, but he stayed calm. He'd never lost an engine before, but there were ways to handle the situation. He flipped a series of switches designed to restart the motor, but none of them worked.

Okay, he told himself, time for Plan B.

If the engine wouldn't reengage, Olsen's only hope was to glide the plane in lazy circles toward the ground and make an emergency landing. By using the wing flaps and other instruments, he could slow the speed of the aircraft and still walk away. At the same time, though, the plane could catch a wrong current and plummet to the ground.

"God!" He called the name out loud, and he heard the fear in his voice. "If You're real, help me. I'm not ready to go."

Two minutes passed in textbook fashion, but then, as Olsen had feared, a strong current dropped the right wing of the plane and the craft began to tumble. Olsen had another thousand feet to go before hitting land, but as the plane fell, he spotted a lake. *Water*, he thought. *That's my only hope.* Landing in the trees or on the hilly ground would cause the Cessna to disintegrate upon impact.

"Water. God, if You're listening, lead me to

the water."

The ground was rushing up to meet him. Suddenly his plane fell to the left and Olsen could see he was going to hit the small lake. The last thing he remembered was the sound of water breaking over his plane and the rush of ice-cold wetness filling the cabin. Suddenly the craft jolted to a stop, and Olsen smacked his head on the doorframe.

After that, there was only darkness.

Bonner was pouring himself a glass of iced tea when he saw a small plane tumble into view and free-fall into the lake at the edge of his property.

"Angela, quick! Call 911. A plane just crashed into the lake."

After years of outdoor training and living, Bonner had always been in good shape. But the cancer medication had taken its toll, and as he ran toward the lake he could barely catch his breath. Fifty yards, a hundred, two hundred, and finally he reached the shore.

The situation was more grim than he'd thought.

The wing of the plane jutted out of the water, but it was otherwise buried in a section of the lake some ten feet deep and seventy-five yards off shore. No one else must have seen the crash, because he was the only one standing at the water's edge looking for signs of life. His heart raced within him, and he still hadn't caught his breath. But he had no choice. Whoever was in the plane was drowning even at that very moment. Before he jumped in, he uttered a silent prayer: *God, if I don't make it back to shore, let Angela know how much I love her.*

Then he dove in and headed as hard and fast as he could toward the plane. Because of his weakened condition, the swim took Bonner twice as long as it normally would have. After five minutes, he reached the wing and though his lungs were already burning from the effort, he sucked in as much air as he could and dove down. His heart pounded, filling his senses with an urgency that drove him deep, deeper toward the fuselage door. He tried twice to open it, and finally on the third try, the door swung free.

Bonner was out of air.

He swam to the surface, nauseated from the effort, grabbed another breath, and went back down. This time he found the pilot in seconds and felt around until he was sure the person was alone. Feeling as though he could die at any moment, Bonner dragged the unconscious man to the surface. They weren't out of danger yet, and that terrified Bonner because, simply, he was out of energy.

Help me, God. Help me. Bonner let the words play in his mind again and again as he kept himself and the man afloat. It took no time to realize that the pilot wasn't breathing.

Swimming with a strength that wasn't his own, Bonner dragged the pilot back to shore. On the beach, despite his exhaustion, he managed to administer CPR. He was three minutes into the process when an emergency crew arrived and took over. He barely made it to the edge of a grove of trees before he dropped to the ground, unable to go on.

At almost the same time, Angela came running toward him. "Bonner!" She waved down one of the paramedics and Bonner heard her explain about his cancer. "Help him, please."

The emergency worker moved quickly and hooked Bonner up to intravenous fluids. They took him to the local hospital, and four hours later he was ready to go home. Before he left, he heard the news about the pilot. The CPR had saved his life.

Bonner figured that might be the end of the situation, but the next day he received a visit from the pilot.

"My name's Olsen Matthews. You saved my life." The man shook Bonner's hand. "The paramedics said you were praying out loud, thanking God at the scene."

"Yes." Bonner stared at the man. He looked wonderful, considering he should have died in the plane crash. "My wife and I were both praying."

The man's eyes grew watery. "Thank you for that." He motioned toward Bonner's house. "Could I come in?"

The two talked for almost an hour. Olsen explained that he'd heard from his doctors about Bonner's cancer. "I have a check for you, something to help with your medical costs." The man shrugged and gave Bonner a slight smile. "Maybe it'll help you get the care you need."

Then Olsen asked Bonner about God. And, with Angela at his side, Bonner told him about their faith and about living a life right before God. At the end of the conversation, Olsen and Bonner prayed.

"Could you be my friend, Bonner? Someone I could visit now and then, someone to talk to about God?"

A smile lifted the corners of Bonner's mouth. He squeezed Angela's hand. "Definitely."

"Good." Olsen stood to leave. "I was asking God about a friend when I crashed. And now He's worked everything out." Olsen walked to the door, looked over his shoulder, and grinned. "I think He's going to work everything out for you, too, Bonner."

When the man was gone, Bonner turned to Angela and remembered the check. "He gave me something, a thank-you gift."

"Well, open it up." Angela stood beside him, peering at the folded check.

Bonner did, and both he and Angela fell silent, shocked.

The check was for one million dollars. In the note section it read only, "Use this to get better."

Bonner did just that. In the months that followed, he tried the costly experimental treatment. Three years later, in one of their many times together, Bonner and Olsen agreed that God had done more than take part in the miracle of Olsen's rescue and Bonner's healing. He also gave them the miracle of new friendship.

Delayed

by Debra Davis

.... ⌇ ....

The woman at the airline ticket counter in Munich, Germany, just shook her head. "I'm sorry, but there's no more availability on this flight," she said. *Great*, I thought. My husband, Bob, and I had enjoyed every moment of our dream vacation—two weeks in Europe—but I was ready to go home to Shreveport, Louisiana, and sleep in my own bed.

Bob could see how frustrated I was. "We'll just have to try to get on the flight tomorrow," he said. "Let's enjoy the extra day."

Bob's right, I thought. There were more important things to be worried about—my son Joe, a First Lieutenant in the Army 82nd Airborne Division, would be returning to Fort Bragg in North Carolina for a short R&R from his tour of duty in Baghdad, and we weren't sure we'd be able to see him in the little time he'd be stateside. Plus the time was so up in the air! Back at our hotel, I checked my e-mail to see if our daughter-in-law Monica had any news on when Joe was due to arrive. Sure enough, there was a message. "Joe's been delayed again," it read, with one of those little frowny faces.

The next morning we made it onto our flight back to the States. Unfortunately, we had to stop in Atlanta. Our connecting flight there was delayed because of bad weather. The hours passed. I felt the frustration building. "That's it!" I finally said. "I just want to get home already!"

That's when I saw a group of soldiers coming down the ramp from one of the gates. I thought of Joe. They're coming back from a war, I reminded my-self. I'm coming back from vacation. What right do I have to be frustrated? Maybe the troops were God's way of reminding me to trust in his time.

Bob grabbed my arm. "Look at those soldiers coming down the ramp."

"I see them," I said.

Bob persisted. "Do you see who's in front?" Suddenly, all those delays across all those miles made perfect sense. I rushed toward my son Joe's open arms.

Finding the Strength to Overcome

by Renie Szilak Burghardt

When I moved to this beautiful, hilly rural area from a city twenty-two years ago, I was finally realizing a lifelong dream. My children were grown and living lives of their own; it was finally my turn to live a life of my own, surrounded by God's beautiful nature. And I have done just that, roaming these hills and woods at will, enjoying the wildlife, and teaching my grandchildren about them whenever they come to visit from the city. It was a life I loved and hoped to continue for some time.

Then one day this past December, my life changed in an instant! We had a light snowfall the day before. Only a couple of inches of snow, but it was enough to make things slippery outside. It was a Saturday, and earlier that day my friend, Jan, and I had an enjoyable time eating lunch at a restaurant and shopping in a large department store. I got home later than usual and rushed to feed the animals.

It was very late afternoon when I noticed the bird feeders needed refilling. Cardinals, chickadees, gold and purple finches, and a multitude of other birds were waiting for their supper before they would settle down for another frigid night. I walked up a small hill to get to the feeders, carrying a bag of wild bird seed. Suddenly, I slipped and landed on my right side with a thud!

Of course, I fully expected to get right back up again and continue my walk to the feeders. But when I tried to get up, the worst pain I have ever experienced shot through my right side, making me cry out, and I quickly realized that I was not going to get to the feeders or anywhere else, for that matter!

It was already past four in the afternoon; it would be dark in another hour, and I had no close neighbors who might see me and come to my aid. And I didn't have my cell phone with me, as I'm supposed to at all times, to call someone for help. Panic gripped my heart as I also realized that if I was going to spend the night outside, I might freeze to death! Somehow, I had to find a way to get into the house. Still trying to rely on my own strength, I tried to get up again, with the same results: unbearable pain and no success.

Dear God, I'm in big trouble here, and I need Your help. Only You can help me now. I pray for Your wisdom and strength. Please help me get back into the house. I trust that You will help and sustain me, but whatever happens now, Thy will be done, Heavenly Father, Thy will be done!

Tears welled in my eyes as I prayed. Then, closing my eyes, I lay there a while, feeling the chill of the snow-covered earth beneath me. I slowly resigned myself to the inevitable—spending the night outside.

But suddenly, a soft whisper of a suggestion entered my head. *"Try to crawl into the house. You will have the strength to do it. I will give you the strength."*

Oh, I don't know if I can, Lord. I don't know if I can.

"You can if you try. Trust in Me and try." When I was a little girl, a long time ago, I believed I heard God's voice. I don't think anyone else believed me, but I knew I did. And now, He was speaking to me again, of that I was certain.

I decided to try to crawl up the hill to my front door. Somehow, I managed to move slowly toward my destination. There was a lot of pain with every move, but I kept crawling. It took me an hour to get to my front door, but as darkness descended I finally was able to make it into the warm house. Exhausted, I lay on the floor for a few minutes and rested.

Finally, I moved again, reaching the sturdy wooden chair in the dining room. I managed to pull myself up, holding onto its back. On the table lay my cell phone. With shaking hands, I reached for it and punched in my son Greg's number.

"I'm hurt. I think I broke my hip. I need help!" I cried into the phone in an anguished voice when he answered. "I'm in so much pain, I can barely stand it." Fifteen minutes later, a sheriff's deputy car and an ambulance pulled into my driveway. Greg, who lives two hundred miles from me, was on his way.

"The door is unlocked," I called out as I heard someone knocking. I was still standing in the dining room, holding onto the wooden chair with all my might. Within minutes I was in the ambulance, speeding toward the hospital and help. The kind woman attendant gave me a pain pill and asked me how and where I fell.

"I was outside, trying to fill the bird feeders, and slipped in the snow," I told her.

"Outside? But how did you manage to get back into the house?" she asked incredulously.

"When I realized I couldn't make it in on my own, I prayed for help. God gave me the strength to make it into the house," I said, grateful tears rolling down my cheeks. "Sometimes it takes a crisis to make one realize once again that God is always near, and all we have to do is ask for His help. He will never let us down." The woman attendant in the ambulance nodded and stroked my head gently.

And now, just a few months after my accidental fall, as I am still recovering from hip surgery, I thank Him daily for being there whenever I need Him. With His help, I am even able to walk again without the aid of a walker, although a small limp still remains to remind me of what transpired: a true miracle. But, according to my doctor, the limp will also be gone, soon enough, and I'll be as good as new. And I have God to thank, for the rest of my days.

SOMEONE WATCHING OVER US

by Linda Roth

———— ⁓⁓ ————

I shushed the kids. Driving in this snow was nerve-racking enough. I was emotionally drained anyway. It was the first Christmas since Jim, my husband, passed away, and I wondered how I could take care of our kids. Even this simple trip to the grocery meant that the three of them—seventeen-year-old CJ, eleven-year-old Sandie, and three-year-old Ronnie—had to come with me. Now, returning home, I couldn't even enjoy the beauty of our snow-covered neighborhood. It just meant shoveling the driveway, salting the front steps, things Jim used to do. Now who would watch out for us?

Better back into the driveway, I thought as I pulled up to the house. It would be easier to unload the groceries and less difficult getting out in the morning. I backed in and put the car in park. "Okay, you kids get out of the cold and go inside. I'll bring in the groceries," I said. I watched till the kids were inside then opened the door and took a step out. I nearly fell on the icy driveway. *That's all I'd need. Better back up a little closer to the house,* I thought. The less distance I had to carry the groceries, the better. I got back in, put the car in reverse and pressed down on the gas pedal. The car didn't budge. The wheels just spun. I shifted gears, tried to pull the car forward then back, rocking it like I'd seen Jim do so many times. Still stuck. *Great. Did my car have to give me problems too? Weren't things difficult enough?* Exasperated, I got out.

That's when Sandie stood up from directly behind the car. "Hi, Mom! I'm helping you get unstuck!" she exclaimed innocently. "I've been pushing."

"Never do that, Sandie!" I scolded, heart racing. *Dear Lord, what if....* I made sure she was safely inside the house before giving it one more try. Again I put the car in reverse. This time, without hesitation, it backed up.

Who would watch out for us? I knew the answer.

A Divine Detour

by Lynn Seely

I had no idea that my decision to live in Scotland for a while would allow God to use me in a dramatic way, but it did.

I was living in the northern part of Scotland in the village of St. Combs. The village had been perched near the edge of the North Sea since 1785. Only a modest cliff overlooking a bare stretch of sand and sea grass lay between my cottage window and the moody sea that, each winter, boiled up furious, frothy white caps and flung howling winds along a chastised coast. In the more temperate seasons, beautiful blue skies counterbalanced the tranquil turquoise swells that licked the sandy shore as if apologizing for their winter wrath.

Two glass bottles of cold milk were delivered each morning to my cozy stone cottage. Each bottle had two inches of fresh thick cream at the top, just waiting beneath a gold foil cap. I'd pour part of the heavy cream into my first cup of hot tea and go outside. I'd sit on the front steps of the cottage in my old fuzzy slippers and faded bathrobe while I watched the darkness fade. Then the sun would gently diffuse the early morning mist and gradually layer the sky in delicate salmon hues.

I would often take long drives in the Scottish Highlands—gliding slowly by sweet heather and lush, grassy meadows that were neatly divided by ancient stone fences. The afternoon sun painted the green hilltops bright gold, leaving the lower slopes in dark olive contrast. It was always peaceful and beautiful, and I never tired of seeing what was around the next bend in the road.

One particular day I was heading home after a leisurely drive in the countryside and although I was near home and had driven this part of the route many times, for some reason I ended up lost. I knew I would need to find a place to turn around, though I wasn't in any hurry to do so. As I drove around a curve, I came upon an accident that had taken place. A huge backhoe was on its side. It had fallen off a trailer when the truck driver tried to negotiate the curve. I saw a woman had been injured and was sprawled on the ground. A group of people stood around her, clearly distressed at her condition.

I pulled my car over to the side of the road and wondered if I should do anything. After all, I had absolutely no training in first aid and I didn't think I could help. Even so, I felt a need to walk over to the scene. I heard someone say that the ambulance had just been called and was on the way, but I knew the nearest one was in Aberdeen, some thirty miles away.

I knelt down beside the woman. She had a huge gaping wound in one arm that cut all the way to the bone. She had already lost a great deal of blood. No one seemed to know what to do except reassure her help was on the way. I knew she needed more than reassuring words or the ambulance would end up transporting a dead body. I felt a paralyzing dread for the woman. I silently prayed and asked God what I should do.

The moment I did, a sure and certain calm came over me, and in an instant I remembered a scene from a TV movie where a tourniquet had been used. I knew exactly what had to be done.

I ran back to my car, grabbed an old ice scraper, broke the handle off, and raced back to the victim's side. One man in the crowd wore a big red handkerchief around his neck. "I need that—now!" Without hesitating, he handed it to me. I soon had a crude tourniquet in place on the woman's arm. I gently twisted the handle—it worked! It seemed like hours, yet it was only ten or fifteen minutes more until the emergency crew arrived. As soon as they were at her side, I stepped back. I prayed that the woman would live.

Just before the ambulance left, one member of the crew said, "You know, you probably saved her life." I didn't mention to him that I had no medical training at all and I had only seen a tourniquet being used once in a TV movie. As I drove home that day I realized if I had not taken the wrong route, I would not have been anywhere near the accident scene.

Two weeks later I went back to the scene of the accident. As I rounded the curve, I saw her. She was sitting in a chair in front of her cottage. Her arm was in a cast from fingertips to shoulder. As I walked up to the woman, her puzzled face suddenly brightened. "Well, now, I don't know your name, but I know your face."

She turned to her husband who had just come out the front door. "It's her! She's the one that bound me up!" They both believed it was a miracle that she had not been killed instantly. I agreed.

"I think you should know something," I said. "I

don't have any medical training at all. I said a prayer at the accident scene right after I got there—and I asked God what I should do. It was the answer to that prayer that saved your life. That is how I knew what to do that day."

I continued, "As for the miracle of my showing up, it is more of a miracle than you know. I was on my way home on a road I know very well, and yet I somehow managed to get lost. If that had not happened… well, I wouldn't have been there at all that day."

I know there are times when the road I plan to travel on—both literally and figuratively—may not be the road I end up on. God may have a detour planned, but there's always a reason.

Mysterious SOS

by Thomas Coverdale

———— ⟋⟍⟍ ————

Vietnam, December 14, 1967—just before the first Tet Offensive. I was with Charlie Company, First Battalion, 25th Lightning Division, near Saigon. In the afternoon a Vietcong death squad hit us, leaving ten dead. At sundown, feeling jittery, I went on patrol. Gribbit, Vigor, and I set up a listening post about five hundred meters from camp. At 1:00 am, I reported in: "This is Charlie, LP One. Lots of movement out here."

The radio on my back crackled: "Get down... we're going to fire." Our guys started throwing rockets into the bush; the enemy started their own barrage. We were pinned down. *Oh, God! Get us out of here...please!* I prayed as I chewed dirt.

There was a thud, like someone punching my

back. A grenade exploded. I felt blood trickling down my back. "We've been hit," I radioed, "we're coming in!" In spite of our wounds, we scrambled in the darkness through a field of claymore mines and hales of razor-sharp wire and stumbled into the arms of the arriving medics.

Three weeks later, when all three of us were out of the hospital and back at camp, my platoon sergeant called me in. "Coverdale, how did you guys manage to let the medics know you'd been hit?"

"Radio, sir." I was surprised he should ask.

"Not with this, soldier," he replied, holding up a twisted, blackened box. It was the radio I had carried on my back. It had taken the full blast of the grenade, probably saving my life. And in doing so, the batteries, the crystal—every component—had been destroyed.

How did the medics get my SOS? I don't know. But God does.

Nowhere Else to Go

by Donnie Galloway

———

Mile after lonely mile, I kept thinking of my cousin. The thoughts were submerged, hidden down deep, and I tried not to pay them any mind. I talked on my CB some, read all the signs for Stuckey's and Fieldcrest, and furniture outlets posted on US Interstate 85, stopped off for a bite to eat at Darrell's Barbecue in Rockwell, North Carolina.

But, like a magnet, my mind kept coming back to my cousin. We'd been close, he and I. Two weeks before, he had killed himself. His suicide stunned me, and inside I felt a heaviness, like a weight, tight, in my chest.

Sad and puzzled, I remembered back to some of those times we'd hung around together. We'd talked for hours, about this or that. He was young. Life was before him, but....

Death. We'd never talked about that.

It had been raining off and on, and the grayness of the day seemed to play on my mind. I was driving south, hauling a load of bricks from Lewis Run, Pennsylvania, to Baton Rouge, Louisiana. I'd been running heavy freight for ten years, ever since I was eighteen.

As my trusty semi and I pushed our way into my home territory of North Carolina, those thoughts of death traveled with me. I remembered grimly that I hadn't even been able to go to his funeral. My mother had to tell me about it. The company I drove for wouldn't let me off. And I'd been asked to be a pallbearer.

It was sprinkling as I pulled out of the weigh station south of Charlotte. I was about to undergo a great change. If only my cousin had still been alive and riding with me that day. His life might have changed, just as mine did.

Just ahead was the Catawba River Bridge, a span of 175 yards. As I drove onto the bridge, an orange sign announced: RIGHT LANE CLOSED—1000 FEET AHEAD. I waited for a lady in a small car to pass, then I pulled over into the left lane behind her.

Suddenly, right in front of me, all of the cars had stopped. But I couldn't! Five tons of metal and eleven tons of bricks were going to smash right into all those people. *Oh, no, dear God, I'm going to kill all of them!* my mind screamed.

There's nowhere else to go, I thought desperately, pulling the wheel hard to the right. In a split second, I knew I had to drive off the bridge. It was either that or kill everyone in front of me.

As I swerved and drove to the edge of the bridge, I heard metal crash into metal. Then I was through the guardrail and falling...the truck and the bricks and I plunging eighty feet through the air. I was terrified. *This is it,* I thought.

We hit the river hard, and the windshield burst. Muddy water gushed in and swept me back into the sleeper. The truck sank the thirty-five feet to the river bottom in a hurry. I was dazed, and my sleeping gear and tools and everything I owned floated around me, confusing me. I couldn't see.

I groped through the blackness. My clothes and boots felt like lead. My lungs were about to burst. I'd never get out of there.

I touched the steering wheel. Beyond was the open windshield and I struggled to it just as the truck began flipping over in a slow arc. Soon my opening would be lying against the river bottom, and I'd be trapped.

I kicked and pushed. I pulled myself through. But then I was lost. I felt as if I were in a tomb, surrounded by choking blackness. Which way was up? I didn't know. I just stretched out my arms and swam.

And then my head hit the river bottom. That's when I gave up. I did say some prayers. It was my time to die.

Dear God, if You want me to live, or if You want me to die, please go with me. And, dear God, help those people on the bridge. Don't let anyone be hurt. Please.

I gave up to whatever was going to happen. And I didn't feel afraid anymore.

Then I felt my body lifting up...and up and up—ten feet, twenty, thirty, thirty-five. I was being pushed up. I broke onto the surface, and there was a boat with two fishermen motoring toward me!

I gasped and choked and hollered, and went under a couple of times, but I fought my way back to the top. I was still alive! I fought to stay afloat until those fishermen grabbed me and pulled me into their boat.

I lay on the bottom of the boat gasping and coughing, gulping in small breaths of air. It felt good, breathing in life again.

Then I managed to say, "Did I hurt anyone? Is everyone okay?"

We looked up at the bridge deck. There were flashing lights. Troopers and wreckers. Crowds of people looking down at us. I gulped. There was an ambulance. *Somebody must have gotten hurt bad*, I thought. For just a second, living didn't feel so good anymore.

The two men with me in the boat yelled up to the bridge, asking if anyone else was hurt. Then I heard the answering voice. "Everybody's okay up here. We called an ambulance for the trucker."

"How is the trucker?" someone shouted from the bridge.

"A bit winded, but he's in pretty good shape!"

Good shape.

Well, one of my legs may never be the same, and my back gives me some trouble now, but I'm still hauling heavy loads on an eighteen-wheeler flatbed truck. And I still drive sometimes over the Catawba River Bridge. There's a patch in the guard rail where I drove through that day, and that patch reminds me of the lesson I learned down on the bottom of that river. I learned something special about life.

I learned it while I was facing death. I knew down there that I would never be afraid of death, but I also discovered something else, something that my cousin could have learned, but didn't: You don't need to be afraid of life, either. Because if you'll just reach

out and ask God to go with you, He'll lift you up and
walk with you the rest of the way.

God has a purpose for each one of us. He wants us
to live, and He'll give us the courage to live if we just
give Him the chance.

An Invisible Shield

by Genovieva Sfatcu Beattie

———— ⁓〰⁓ ————

*I*n 1979, when Romania was still under the repressive regime of Nicolae CeauÐescu, Sunday school was against the law and children were supposed to sing only Communist songs. At the time, I directed a youth choir at a Baptist church in Iasi, Romania's second-largest city. We continually faced hurdles such as having to rehearse in an old woodshed or out in the forest where we could escape the police. I often told the youngsters God would provide His protection.

I found out how this worked on a trip we made to Vicovu de Sus, a small mountain village. We stayed at the home of one of our hosts, and the only place big enough for the fifty of us to rehearse was his backyard.

"First we must pray for safety," I said before we warmed up with a musical version of the twenty-third Psalm. We were singing "I will fear no evil..." when a black car pulled up and a policeman in a blue uniform got out.

"I have orders to arrest you," he said to me.

"I can't come," I said. "I'm responsible for these children." *Lord, help us.* Two of the girls clutched my skirt, and the youngest boy held my hand.

"Hurry up. Let her go!" the policeman shouted. I began hugging the youngsters one by one, saying farewell. By then the policeman was speaking into his walkie-talkie. Soon another car arrived, a shiny black one with three aerials. Two men in suits and dark glasses got out. The dreaded secret police. "Comrade," the tall one said, "you are under arrest."

The children clutched me even closer and moved in a tight circle around me. The policemen claimed they would bring me back soon, but the boys and girls only pressed harder. "Come at once," one officer said.

"I cannot move," I answered. "You come and get me."

And then something amazing happened. For a

minute at least, no one moved. The police seemed rooted to the ground. They came no closer. It was as though an invisible shield had gone up around me and the children. After a few minutes, the policemen went back to their cars. They got in, slammed the doors, and took off in a cloud of dust.

At the concert that evening, the children sang more beautifully than ever before.

Menaced by a Mad Bull

by Gene Fleenor

---

*I*t was a Sunday afternoon in mid May, when I went to check the herd I keep on a spread just north of town. Heavy rains a couple of days earlier had washed some vegetation into the cows' pasture. The cows became listless, so I turned them into the east pasture away from the vegetation, figuring it had soured their stomachs.

Normally I loved going over to the farm, especially on a warm spring day. But not that day. Dr. J. Nathan Wilson, who had fused ruptured disks in my back the year before, had just advised me that not only would I have to quit my job and go on disability but that I would have to get someone else to tend my cattle. My back was too fragile for the physical work of cattle ranching. I felt I was losing everything I loved.

I also worked as a supervision officer for Lubbock

County, overseeing probationers and helping them adjust to life out of jail. I had been a policeman in Lubbock for five years and had become a caseworker after getting a degree in religion from Wayland Baptist University. To me, this job was the perfect combination of my background in law enforcement and my interest in the ministry. Every time one of my probationers made it on the outside, I felt I was doing God's work. But now I was worried about my future and confused. I could reconcile having to turn over my farm chores or selling the farm. But the doctor said that even sitting for hours in my office chair was bad for my back. If God was using me in my work, why was that being taken from me, too?

I stopped my pickup about two hundred and fifty feet from where the cattle were bunched up. As I ducked under the fence, I felt a stab of pain in my lower back. Wearily, I trudged toward the cattle. On the way, about fifty feet from the herd, I noticed the tailgate was open on the livestock trailer I kept in the pasture. I latched it closed then headed toward the herd again. And then, for no apparent reason, I went back and opened the tailgate. I felt weird undoing something I had just done, but I shrugged it off.

As usual, the bull came forward to greet me. Like most bulls, he's a little ornery and more than a little stubborn, but he had never given me any trouble. "Hello, bull," I told him, "I guess you've come to get your ears scratched." I obliged and petted him for a bit, but, noticing the cows were grazing contentedly, I wanted to get over to the barn and turn the calves in for nursing. "All right, bull, go over to the cattle," I said, waving him away. He shuffled backward and was about to turn and trot off when he bumped hard into a stray cow. She bellowed. Momentarily, he was off balance and startled. Then he looked at me, angry.

He put his head down and started coming at me slowly but deliberately. "Git, bull! Go on. Back!" I told him sternly, shooing him with my arms. He kept coming, then dipped his head low and butted me.

"Doggone, bull! Git. Go on!" I backed away and shooed him with my arms again. He butted me and kept advancing. I balled my fist and smacked his nose hard. He just snorted and kept right on shoving and butting me, pushing me about thirty feet past the trailer. I took my eyes off him for a second to calculate how I might make a run for the trailer, and that's when he surged at me. His head bashed into my leg just below the knee.

There was a sickening crunch of shattering bone. Pain flamed up my leg to my neck. The blow knocked my hat and glasses off and sprawled me on my back.

The bull kept coming at me, pawing and butting. Each time he hit me, my left leg flopped around below the knee. I nearly passed out from the pain. I started clawing my way back toward the trailer.

"Oh, God," I cried out, "help me get away from him!"

Somehow I dragged myself the thirty feet to the trailer. Once there, I couldn't raise myself the foot and a half to get up. When I tried to wrench my body in with my arms, my right shoulder seized in pain. It was as useless as my left leg. Desperately, I lunged at the trailer. Suddenly I was inside! The bull must have caught me just right and flipped me in. I scooted around so I could close and latch the tailgate.

Relentlessly the bull battered the trailer, shoving it several times. I was knocked around like a rag doll on the trailer bed, my leg and shoulder flaming with pain. Through the waves of pain, I marveled that I had somehow been flipped into it. I shuddered. If I had left the tailgate latched, I would have been breathing my last about now.

"God," I prayed, "I know you got me to safety in this trailer, but I have to get out of here. You are going to have to get that bull to go somewhere else."

After a time the bull seemed to lose interest and drifted away with the herd. The shattered bones in my lower left leg popped and ground as I shifted my way out of the trailer. Finally I got both legs on the ground, but the pain was so intense I couldn't edge my way out. "Lord, you are going to have to do it. I can't."

Suddenly I was flat on my back. Two hundred feet of bumpy pasture separated me from my truck. Lying on my left side, I was able to inch along, crabbing with my shoulder and pushing with my right leg. I made it about twenty-five feet and stopped, exhausted. My shoulder was on fire with pain, and my leg was throbbing, swollen and stretching my pant leg. The hundred and seventy five feet I had to go might as well have been a hundred and seventy five miles.

"God," I said again, "I can't make it. You're going to have to send someone to help me."

A voice played in my mind: *"Who do you think you're talking to?"* It was not audible, but it was plain as day that God had spoken to me—not loud or angry, but commanding.

Taken aback with fear and wonder, I answered, "I'm talking to you, God. I can't make it without someone's help."

"I am here."

I got the message. I began crabbing along again, stopping every five feet or so to rest. Each time

I paused, I heard, *"I am with you."* With endurance beyond my own, I finally scooted under the fence to the pickup. I stared at the door handle. From where I was lying in the dirt road's ruts, it looked a mile high. I twisted my back up against the side of the truck, but when my hand grasped the handle I couldn't open the door because all my weight was leaning against it. If I fell, I knew I would pass out from the pain. "Oh, God, I've got to get this door open some way."

Next thing I knew I was leaning against the truck's seat with the door open. I got inside, but I couldn't drag my left leg in. I put the truck in gear and slowly drove to the nearest neighbor's house, keeping the door open with my left hand and steering with my right. The truck bounced along the rutted road, wracking my leg with pain. I began to lose consciousness. I pulled up near the neighbor's front door and leaned on the horn, but no one came. I had to get myself to the hospital, fifteen miles away.

I managed to reach the seat release lever and push the seat back. I inched my bad leg in and fastened my seat belt to keep myself upright. I don't remember much about the trip to the hospital except that underlying the terrible pain there was an assurance that came from beyond: *"I am in control."* I felt more like a spectator than driver. The truck stopped a time or two at lights, then made a U-turn to get on the access road to Saint Mary Hospital. I believe the Holy Spirit was driving that truck more than I was.

Two men standing outside alerted the emergency room staff. After I was on a gurney and being wheeled in, I let myself sink below the haze of pain into unconsciousness.

The next days passed in a blur of numbed pain. On Tuesday, Dr. Wilson pieced my shattered leg back together with a metal plate and twenty screws. When I came to after the operation, I felt strange.

That Thursday when my wife Nita came to visit, I was picking at my lunch. I told her, "I should be happy just to be alive and that Dr. Wilson saved my leg, but I feel so out of kilter. I don't know what's wrong with me."

"Well, you do have a lot to be thankful for, you—" Nita began.

I felt like I had been hit by a lightning bolt. Suddenly I was back in the pasture latching the trailer tailgate and heading toward the herd. Then I felt the same weird nudge that made me go back and unlatch the tailgate—the nudge that saved my life.

"That's it!" I fairly shouted. "Nita, I left God back in the pickup truck when I got to the hospital. I haven't been listening for him and I haven't been thankful. That's what's been the matter with me these past few days." Right then I started to pray, "Lord, I'll never leave you out of my life like that again."

Immediately I felt right.

Sure enough, I had to go on disability and get out of cattle farming. I needed three more surgeries after that first one to get my leg and shoulder right. Even now, I'm not able to move around much. I can sit and stand only for short periods of time. But there is peace in my heart. I have learned to trust God in all things. I used to pray, "This is what I want, Lord, please bless it."

Now I say, "Your will, not mine." Then I put my mind at ease. If God can remove me from the path of an angry bull, then I don't need to worry about tomorrow. God will take care of all my tomorrows in His own perfect way.

"MIJO, THE LORD WILL PROVIDE"

by Isaac J. Canales

⎯⎯⎯⎯⎯⎯⎯⎯⎯

It was the one day of the year Mama didn't put beans and tortillas or even her specialty—tamales—on the table. When it came to celebrating Thanksgiving, we were as American as anybody else. Cranberry sauce, pumpkin and mincemeat pies, turkey, mashed potatoes and gravy—all that and stuffing too. Mama made the best.

But the year I was eleven, we hadn't even begun our holiday preparations by the time the end of November rolled around. And I knew why.

Papa and Mama were pastors of a little church in Keystone (now Carson), California. We were poor—so poor our rent in the projects, twenty-six dollars a month, was almost more than we could handle. We lived on whatever the congregation could afford to give. That fall, times were hard for everyone, and offerings hit an all-time low. I watched the tambourine we used for a collection plate very, very closely.

Nervously I asked Mama about our Thanksgiving dinner. "Isaac, God will provide," she replied. "You know He has always been faithful to us." I remembered the shoes, winter coats, even parts for the family car that had arrived just when we needed them. Maybe Mama was right. But time was running out. I waited anxiously for something to happen.

Soon the holiday was upon us. I could hear the tambourine rattle dully as a few meager coins hit the skin. *Why hasn't God stepped in?* I wondered.

I asked Mama again if we would have turkey. "*Mijo*," she said (meaning "my son"), "the Lord will provide. Has He ever let us down?"

That kept me quiet until Tuesday. Papa and I went to McCoy's Market for groceries to get us through the week—a dozen eggs, tortillas, milk. While he was at the checkout, I hurried to the meat department to look at the "toms," as Mama called them. Wistfully I ran my hand over the plump, frozen birds. It wouldn't be Thanksgiving without a turkey.

Wednesday night we gathered in our church, a gutted two-bedroom house with a sign in black-and-yellow letters that read MISIÓN EBENEZER ASAMBLEA DE DIOS. I watched the regulars assemble: Sister Ayala, with her colorful shawl draped around her shoulders; Brother Garcia, who worked in the orchards; and Sister Audrey, a six-foot-two-inch, seventy-two-year-old former B-movie extra who played the violin and wore a dark fur coat. My family and a few others made up the rest of the congregation that evening.

I tugged on Mama's sleeve as she headed up to the little blue pump organ next to the pulpit. "I know there won't be enough for Thanksgiving dinner," I said. "What are we going to do?"

"Shh," she whispered, looking serene as always. "Don't worry, mijo, the Lord will provide." If that were true, wouldn't He have done something by now?

The service began. Mama played the organ, Papa strummed the guitar, and Sister Audrey joined in on her violin as we sang "There Is Power in the Blood" in Spanish. Papa spoke about the holiday being a time to give thanks to the Lord for His provision. Then he called me: "Isaac, would you please pick up the tithes and offerings tonight? And would you ask the Lord to bless them?"

It was an honor to be asked to participate in the service, but it was the last thing I wanted that night. I mumbled a prayer for the few coins I knew were all that would be forthcoming. After I said amen and raised my head, my eyes caught the glitter of a shiny black car pulling up in front of the church. It was the longest and newest car I had ever seen. The door opened and a tall, handsome man dressed in a tuxedo stepped out. He looked like Clark Gable, right down to his pencil-thin mustache. He came in and sat in the second pew. I could tell by the puzzled glances that the whole congregation wondered who he was.

I'm sure Mama played offertory music that night, but all I could hear was the thud of the coins as they dropped into the tambourine. I slowly worked my way around the room toward the elegant stranger until finally I stood directly in front of him.

A hint of a smile played around his lips. He reached into his jacket pocket, pulled out a cloth napkin and slipped it onto the tambourine. It was so heavy that I had to steady the tambourine with both hands. "Thank you!" I croaked as I watched twenty silver dollars roll out of the napkin.

Returning to the front of the church, I could not contain my happiness. Mama was staring at me curiously. I pointed to the tambourine and mouthed *turkey*. She didn't look surprised; she just smiled and launched into a rousing rendition of "When the Saints Go Marching In."

The stranger slipped out before the service ended, before anyone could ask who had sent him. I didn't have to ask. I knew. The next evening, as Papa asked the blessing for our Thanksgiving feast, I silently added a prayer of my own: *Thank You, God, for always being faithful. From now on, I'll try to be too.* Mama's turkey and dressing had never tasted better.

Mama is in heaven now. I am the pastor of Papa's church. We have grown to more than one thousand members and have a beautiful new church building only three blocks from that two-bedroom house. I still sometimes worry about how our needs will be met, especially since my wife and I have three teenage sons. Then I hear Mama's whisper in my ear, "Don't worry, mijo. The Lord will provide." And He does. Not always as dramatically as that long ago Thanksgiving eve, but just as surely.

2
POWER FROM HEAVEN

*I*t is God who works in you to will and to act in order
to fulfill his good purpose.

PHILIPPIANS 2:13 NIV

*Thank You, Lord, for the power You have to renew us
and transform our lives. We give You all praise and honor and glory!*

Opened Eyes

by Cheryl Pietromonaco

———————— ·⁄∖∖⁄· ————————

One thing troubled me about my husband: He didn't believe in God. "Believe what you like," he said, "but there isn't someone up there making miracles happen." I prayed hard for him to come around. That would definitely take a miracle.

One winter we took a vacation in the Montana mountains. His brother owned a cabin there and lent us his Jeep—"You'll need the four-wheel drive," he said. He handed us a large key ring, indicating the key for the Jeep and the one for the cabin. We arrived late in the afternoon. I was awed by the isolation, the delicate, powdery snow frosting everything in sight and the utter silence. We dropped our bags, took off our coats and my husband tossed the keys onto the kitchen table. They landed with a metallic clank. I needed a drink, but there was no running water. "Let's grab a bucket; we'll get some water from the creek," my husband said. We left the door open to clear the musty air while we were out.

We weren't far when a strong gust of wind blew. There was a loud bang. The cabin door! We stopped and stared at each other, thinking the same thing, *I hope that door didn't just lock....* We ran back through the snow. The door was locked tight. "The keys are on the kitchen table!" my husband groaned.

He rammed a shoulder against the door. It didn't budge. "See if there's a wire or something in the Jeep," he told me. "Maybe we can pick the lock."

"I'll say a prayer too," I told him.

Nothing of help was in the glove compartment or seat pockets. I searched and prayed. Under the driver's seat, I felt something and fished it out. A ring of keys! Just like the set my brother-in-law gave us. I rushed back to the cabin. Sure enough, one of the keys opened the door. Saved!

My husband looked at the table. The keys he'd tossed on it were gone! We looked for that first ring of keys, but never found another set.

Later, my brother-in-law insisted the key ring he'd handed us was the only set he had. "I just don't get it," my husband said, confused. But I did. I got the miracle I'd asked for.

The cabin door wasn't the only thing opened up that day. My husband's eyes finally started to open as well.

Brought Together

by Allen van Meter

"God, please, no!" I wanted to cry out that night when my sister called and told me what happened to my nephew Michael. He had suffered a gunshot wound to the head. A careless accident, but the damage was massive and irreversible. Only machines were keeping him alive. "Come home," my sister whispered as she hung up. "Help us." I would have done anything for her and Michael, but even as my wife, Marilyn, grabbed the phone and started calling airlines, trying to get us seats on the next flight to Kentucky, I couldn't quite bring myself to believe he was gone.

Michael was my sister's son. His father wasn't in the picture, so I was the one who looked out for him and took him fishing when he was little. I tried so hard to protect him from the rough-and-tumble life of the Kentucky backwoods, the life that would have destroyed me if the Lord hadn't come to my rescue. I'd even had Michael live with Marilyn and me in Florida when his teenage rebelliousness got to be too much for my sister to handle. He was a lot like me, the good and the bad. Hardheaded yet bighearted, a taste for living on the edge mixed with a bedrock belief in the value of hard work. Both Michael and I grew a lot in those years together—he because our boys looked up to him like a big brother; I because I knew he was looking to me for an example.

Memories played through my mind like an old, grainy home movie. Little Michael jumping up and down with his first catch from the creek. Michael gleefully (and skillfully) driving a front loader before he was old enough to get his learner's permit. Michael working three jobs at once, then zooming around on his motorcycle after hours. Michael calling us just a few days ago so excited, like a kid on Christmas morning, about finding God. He was only twenty-five. How could it all be taken away from him in a single senseless moment? *Lord, this doesn't make sense,* I prayed. *You gave me a second chance. Why not Michael?*

Really, my turnaround was nothing short of a miracle. Back then, I was totally broken from my addictions to alcohol and drugs. The crime I'd turned to in order to support my habit landed me in a Florida prison and forced me to dry out, but it didn't do anything for the self-destructive spiral I was continuing down.

One day, I was slumped on my bunk in my cell, thinking, *I've messed up everything worth caring about. I might as well be dead.* Then a fellow inmate came by. "I'm going to chapel," he said. "You're coming with me." I couldn't muster the energy to argue, so I followed him out of the cell block. I sat way in the back of the chapel like a zombie, not even caring where I was.

All of a sudden a presence spoke to me, the voice cut clear through my despair. *"Allen, if you give Me your life, I'll restore it back to you."* I knew it could only be God. Who else could bring a spiritually dead man back to life?

Through the rest of my sentence, I read the Bible and got to know the Lord. I talked to Him like I'd talk to a friend. "God, let me know what You want me to do," I'd ask. "I'm kind of thickheaded, so You'll probably have to speak real loud and clear to get through to me."

One morning that spring, I was lying on my bunk

with my Bible open on my chest, thinking about my release in September. Again, I felt the presence I'd felt in chapel and heard a direct message: *"Wait until after February 14 to get married. I will bring her to you."* That sure came out of the blue! I hadn't given marriage much thought because I figured it would be next to impossible to find a woman willing to share her life with someone who'd messed up his own so bad. I tucked that promise from God away in the back of my mind. First things first, I figured. I was released and went into an aftercare center in Jacksonville, Florida.

I was at an evening service at the church down the road the Sunday after Valentine's Day, sitting in the same pew as two little boys, unable to take my eyes off the blond leading the songs. I'd noticed her that morning at coffee hour, too. Marilyn, the preacher said her name was. *She's the one,* something kept telling me. The singing ended. She came down the aisle and sat down—right in my pew, between me and the boys. She was their mom. The service went on, and the younger boy nodded off. Pretty soon he was stretched out on the pew fast asleep, scooting his mom right up next to me. That was the confirmation I needed. I worked up my nerve and asked Marilyn out for coffee the next night. Not long after that, I asked her to be my wife. Turned out Marilyn, too, had felt the Lord leading us together.

In the ten years since our marriage, we hadn't been apart, and it was at moments like tonight, facing this tragedy in my family, that I was most grateful God had given me Marilyn to lean on.

She hung up the telephone. "Finally, some good news," she said. "I got you on a flight leaving first thing in the morning. You'll change planes in Memphis—"

"Wait," I interrupted her, confused, "aren't you coming with me?"

"There's only one seat left on that plane," she said. "You need to be in it. I'll take a later flight." She must have seen my look of dismay. "Don't worry, Allen, I'll be right behind you."

Right behind me, Lord? I need Marilyn right there next to me!

The phone rang before I could say anything. "The doctors said Michael's brain-dead. They're asking me to donate his organs," my sister sobbed. "Please make the decision. I just can't."

"Donating would be the right thing to do," I said slowly. "At least some good can come out of this. Hang on. I'll be there tomorrow."

Early the following morning Marilyn dropped me off at the airport. I picked up my ticket and went to the gate. "Sir, you're seated in 8B, on the aisle," the flight attendant said. *Lord, I'm leaning on You like always. Tell me what to do. I'll do it. I promise.*

At row 8, a dark-haired woman in a red blazer was trying to get her suitcase into the overhead bin. I gave her a hand. She nodded her thanks, then wordlessly settled into the window seat.

Shortly after takeoff, she pulled some papers out of her purse and studied them intently. I glanced over. They were diagrams of the human body. Maybe she could answer some of my questions about Michael.

"Excuse me," I said, "are you a doctor?"

"No," she sighed. "I'm going over these because my sister's in bad shape, and she needs one of my kidneys."

"I'm sorry to hear that," I said.

"Debbie's been sick for a long time," she said. "With liver disease, actually. She got a transplant, only now her body's rejecting it. She's on the waiting list for another liver, but all the medication she's taking has damaged her kidneys. I'm on my way to her hospital in New Orleans to get tested as a donor."

"I'm headed to Kentucky because my family's going through something similar," I said. "My nephew is being taken off life support. We're going to donate his organs."

"It was good of your family to make the decision to donate."

She went back to her medical diagrams, and I closed my eyes to get some rest. But my mind kept going back to another conversation, the last one I had with Michael. He'd been so awestruck at finding God at work in his life.

God at work…. My eyes flew open. I tapped my seatmate on the shoulder. "I think there's a reason we ended up next to each other. I have a feeling my nephew's liver should go to your sister." As soon as I said that, I sensed the Lord's presence, as real and unmistakable as I had those other times, telling me, *"Yes, this is what I want you to do."*

"It's not that simple," my seatmate said. "There are all kinds of rules. And the blood and tissue types must match."

I stared at the air phone in the seatback before us, the voice of the Lord resounding in my head: *"This is what I want you to do."* "Look, it's more than coincidence," I insisted. "This is definitely God at work here. I feel it. We have to get on that phone right now and find out how to get the liver to your sister."

This time my seatmate didn't argue. She dug out a credit card and a list of numbers, and punched one into the air phone. "This is Jan Larson," she said. "My sister, Deborah White, is on your waiting list for a liver transplant." Jan explained what we were looking to do and listened for a while to the response. Then she turned to me. "The nurse says we can do this. It's called a directed donation. They'll still have to confirm the organ match and be able to get it to New Orleans within ten hours. Can you call the hospital where your nephew is and get things started there?"

I picked up the air phone, dialed, and got through to the nurse in charge of transplant coordination. "My name is Allen Van Meter. My nephew is Michael Gibson. He was declared brain-dead not long ago, and his mother signed the papers to donate his organs. Well, we have a woman in New Orleans we want to give his liver to."

"I'm sorry," the nurse said. "It's too late. They're about to unhook Michael and wheel him into the OR to harvest his organs."

"This is of God!" I practically shouted. "It's not too late!"

Silence. Then I heard the phone being set down and footsteps scurrying away. It seemed like forever before the nurse got back on the line. "It wasn't too late," she said quietly. "I stopped them."

"Jan, we're just in time!" I exclaimed.

At the Memphis airport, Jan and I exchanged numbers. "I can't tell you how much your nephew's gift means. Please thank your sister," she said. "We'll pray for you." She gave me a big hug good-bye and rushed to catch her connecting flight to New Orleans.

Three days later, I was trying to write Michael's eulogy, Marilyn at my side again, when Jan called from New Orleans. "Debbie's doing great," she said. "Your nephew's liver really and truly came just in time." She explained that during the operation, the surgeons discovered Debbie's hepatic artery—the main blood line to the liver—was so clogged that she had only hours to live. If they'd gone ahead with just the kidney transplant as planned, it would have killed her. "Even the doctors say it's a miracle. Debbie was in intensive care for weeks after her first liver transplant. This time she's doing so well that pretty soon she'll be coming to thank you in person. She's been telling everyone Michael and the Lord turned the sunset of her life into a glorious sunrise."

I knew what I would say at Michael's funeral. I would talk about one of his kidneys going to a young father; the other to a little boy. A three-month-old baby got his corneas; a badly burned child, skin grafts. Fifty cancer patients received some of his bone marrow. And, of course, I would tell everyone about how I ended up with the last seat left on that plane, right next to a woman whose sister was in dire need of a transplant. It was all because of the One who helped my family make sense of our tragedy by transforming it into a second chance for so many others.

THE CONTRACT

by Jess Bell

Most people have at least one bad habit they would like to break—be it overeating, nail-biting, or gambling. Likewise, most people have their own favorite method of breaking—or trying to break—a bad habit.

Let me tell you about my bad habit and, more importantly, how I learned to overcome it. Perhaps my method will be of help to you too.

On a snowy February night in Cleveland, Ohio, I was by myself in our quiet house. My wife Julie had gone to bed, and our four children were either away at college or at homes of their own.

Standing at the bar in our family room. I gazed dully at the half-empty glass in my hand. A vague sense of disquiet washed over me as I realized that I was slowly getting smashed.

Why are you doing this? I asked myself accusingly.

What kind of way is this for a supposedly recovered alcoholic to be spending his evening? Such behavior just didn't fit in with my highly visible public image as Jess Bell, fifty-seven-year-old president of Bonne Bell Cosmetics, Inc., as well as community leader, fitness enthusiast, marathon runner, and—lest I forget—regenerate Christian.

While I no longer drank as much as I used to, it bothered me that I was never able to stop altogether. Why was it so hard for me to quit?

For me to drink to any degree was plain stupid—especially when I considered all the troubles that booze had brought me: the near breakup of my marriage and near loss of our family-owned business, founded in 1927 by my late father, Jesse G. Bell, a man of high principles and strong character.

It had been through sheer willpower and a disciplined program of daily running that I had originally gotten off the bottle and pulled my life together. A few years later, through my renewed faith in Christ and in the life-changing power of His Holy Spirit, it would seem that I would never again be tempted to drink to excess.

So what was I doing here, alone, in my own house, slowly getting drunk?

Please, God, I prayed, *You've got to help me. You've*

done it before. I know You can do it again.

Feeling the tiniest flutter of optimism that maybe, with God's help, I really might be able to quit drinking once and for all, I took my glass and emptied it into the nearby sink. *That's it!* I thought as I turned on the tap to rinse away the contents. *I'm not going to drink again.*

I hoped that what I had just done was symbolic of what God might do for me—rinse away my yearning for booze with the cleansing power of His Holy Spirit.

The following morning I awoke with a sense of new resolve and, as I had done so many times before in my battle with alcoholism, made this solemn promise: *Today I am not going to drink.*

For several days, this approach seemed to work. I didn't break my promise. But one morning about two weeks later, I awoke exhausted and anxious.

Today I am not going to drink, I promised myself. But on this particular morning, my pledge seemed flat, empty, without power.

Recalling how many times in the past I had broken promises to myself—especially promises about drinking—I felt even more discouraged and depressed. It occurred to me that if I ever was going to stop drinking completely, sheer willpower and promises to myself weren't enough. I needed outside help.

At that moment, a bright idea broke through my gloom like a ship's flare on a stormy night.

I was a businessman, a good businessman, and proud that when I gave my promise to somebody I never broke it. As such, why couldn't I, as an honorable businessman, address my daily pledge—in a sort of cosmic contract—to God? While I might be tempted to break a promise to myself, I would never consider breaking a promise or contract with another person—especially if that person was God.

The idea so excited me that I could hardly contain myself. "Good morning, God!" I heard myself exclaim. "It's going to be a great day. I'm not going to drink—and I'm going to run!"

The moment the words escaped my mouth, I knew that I was going to honor my promise. Because God was so real to me, and because He loved me enough to send His only Son Jesus to die for me, how could I do otherwise?

More than a year has passed since I first made my daily contract with God. I'm happy to report that I haven't had a drink since, and I have run every day. If you believe in God, and have a habit of your own you'd like to overcome, why not try a daily pledge like mine? You may be pleasantly surprised at the results.

Take it from a guy who knows.

The Loving Arms of God

by Marion Bond West

———— ⁓ ————

For the first time in my life, I didn't care about anyone else in the world except my husband Jerry. And myself. Usually I welcomed the opportunity to become involved in someone's life. But not now.

I eased the car into the special section marked RADIATION THERAPY. The hospital let radiation patients park free. Despite the cold November air, we walked slowly because Jerry couldn't walk fast. Inside the amiliar waiting room, we sat in green leather chairs with others awaiting their daily dose of cobalt. We met there each day, the same people, almost as if we were waiting our turns in a beauty shop or some other normal place.

Jerry always entered the waiting room smiling and made it a point to speak to each person. Inevitably he started a conversation. I'd bought him a warm fur hat since he was bald from the brain surgery that had only partially removed the menacing tumor. Already his memory failed sometimes, and he forgot to remove his hat in the waiting room. I removed it for him, and he didn't seem to mind.

It had been more than two months since that day in September when the first horrendous signs of the disease came crashing down on Jerry. Two massive seizures, he'd had. I told myself that by now I should have become adjusted to the idea that my husband of twenty-five years was walking around with a malignant brain tumor.

But I hadn't. The "adjustment" simply would not come. Hundreds of times I tried to adjust. I tried mentally picturing myself standing in the ocean. It was an actual scene from my childhood, the time a giant wave had caught me suddenly from behind and flung me around and around like a towel in a washing machine. That day in the sea, my feet had touched solid ground at last, but now, in the vivid picture in my mind, as soon as I stood, another giant wave came and then another. They continued to knock me down. They meant to destroy me. I couldn't stand or breathe and I didn't see how I ever would again. Not ever.

Across the waiting room, Jerry sat with two other men. His rich, spontaneous laughter brought me back to reality. Now the man sitting by Jerry was laughing too. The third man leaned way over to join in their conversation. I almost resented Jerry's ability to still be sociable and fun. He never stopped smiling or trying to encourage others. I sat frozen like a store mannequin, staring straight ahead.

"Mr. West," came the familiar soft tone of the nurse's voice calling him over the intercom to the treatment room. I watched carefully to see if he needed my help to get up. No, he was managing alone today. An elderly woman across the room smiled at me. I glanced away, pretending not to see. *You're old,* I thought with resentment. *All the people here are old. We aren't. We are just in our forties.* The waves came crashing in on me mentally, and I couldn't stand or get my breath. I was under the water again, thinking, *All I want in life is to grow old with Jerry. That's all I want.*

I was staring at the beige wall, determined not to let anyone catch my attention or start a conversation, when God spoke to me. It seemed I hadn't heard from Him in so long. God and I used to have daily conversations. Exact words came to me from Him.

Silently, but clearly. And I loved to speak to Him too. But since Jerry's surgery and the grim-faced doctor's report, I hadn't listened for God's gentle voice. And my words to Him seemed stilted, as if we weren't friends anymore. I never stopped hurting or fighting off fear. And God wasn't saying anything. But today, He was speaking. The message from Him came again, loud and clear and as distinct as the nurse calling Jerry over the intercom.

"I want you to go to the woman in the hall and speak to her about Me. She's in a wheelchair. You'll know her. You can see her from where you're sitting. Tell her about Me and that I love her."

There were several women in wheelchairs, but I knew the one. Frail, she had probably been beautiful once. She clutched the sides of the wheelchair with open apprehension. Most of her hair was gone. She had that gaunt, hopeless look. Her bright pink robe didn't do much to make her look cheerful.

I don't want to, I told God. *I don't care about her. She's old and I just don't care. What about Jerry and me?*

"Obey Me. I know what's best for you. Go over now and talk to her."

She's not going to respond. Look at her. She doesn't care either. Neither of us cares about anyone anymore.

"Go on, Marion."

It was one of the most difficult things I'd ever

done, and I'd done some almost impossible things in the last two months. I bent over and spoke softly, "Hello. My name's Marion. What's yours?"

She stared ahead, as though I weren't there.

"Keep trying," the silent voice urged.

I touched her hand. I wasn't in any mood to make small talk. "God loves you."

Very slowly, her cold blue eyes met mine. She turned her head slightly. She spoke softly too. "I don't believe in God."

I wasn't surprised, but something stirred within me. I was beginning to care about her. Just a little. It felt good. "That doesn't keep Him from loving you. God loves you very much. What's your name?"

She moistened her lips with her tongue; it was an effort. "Thelma. I'm dying, you know. I've never believed in God or asked Him for anything, and I won't start now. I'm a stubborn old woman."

"I like you," I said and almost smiled.

"Why?" she gasped.

"Because you're honest. I'll see you tomorrow. Okay?"

She nodded.

Jerry came out of the treatment room, walking that unsteady, confused walk that direct radiation to the brain always caused. I placed the fur hat on him, held his arm, and we left. It always felt good to leave. He was smiling, as always.

I moved about the house in robotic fashion, still trying to imagine standing up as the giant waves washed over me. I couldn't stand against such destruction. It was impossible. No one could. But still I tried to picture it in my mind. The idea was so real to me, and I wondered what it would be like, to be able to stand in those waves.

Finally, it was time to go to bed. It was the only time that my mind rested from the agony of Jerry's illness. Mercifully, I could sleep, and it was a welcome relief. Jerry was already asleep beside me. I'd halfway been trying to think of something I could take to Thelma. A way of saying that God cared about her. Something she could hold on to and take back to her hospital room. I knew by her bracelet that she was a patient in the hospital. I thought of taking her a Bible, or a statue of praying hands. God interrupted my thoughts: *"No, no, no. You don't take something like that to someone who doesn't even believe in Me."*

He was right, of course. I was still debating about backing out of this thing with Thelma. She certainly wasn't encouraging our friendship.

The instructions came quickly: *"Look up in the top of your closet, way back in the left-hand corner under some stuff. Get*

*the beautiful, handmade shawl, the ivory one. Give that to
Thelma and say, 'This isn't a shawl. It looks like a shawl, but
it's not. It's the arms of God, loving you.' Tell her it's from Me.
Then wrap the shawl around her with your arms and hug her,
a little longer than necessary."*

You'd have to know the kind of closet I have to really
appreciate the instructions about the location of the
shawl. I hadn't seen the shawl in several months.
Messy closets have never bothered me, and Jerry
seemed to understand and tolerate my side of the
closet. I didn't turn on the light, just tiptoed to the
closet and reached up on the shelf, way in the back,
left-hand side under some stuff. My hand went right
to the soft, luxurious material, and I pulled it out
with amazement. God and I were really talking again!

The next morning we arrived for Jerry's cobalt at
ten sharp. I looked in the hall at the patients lined up
awaiting treatment. Would Thelma really be there?
She could come anytime during the day. But there
she was in the bright pink robe. I got Jerry seated,
removed his hat, and hurried over to Thelma. "I have
something for you."

"I'm not going to take it. Why should I?" she
snapped. "I don't know you!"

Standing behind her I pulled the shawl from the
bag and carefully placed it around her frail shoul-

ders. I did it slowly and deliberately and enfolded her in my arms…a little longer than necessary. "It's not from me. It's from God. Now it may look like a shawl, but it's not."

I waited a moment. She bit instantly. "Well, what is it then?" Already she was stroking it as one would a kitten.

"It's the arms of God, holding you and loving you."

I came around to the front of her wheelchair. She stared at me, her mouth a small, round O. I seized the unguarded moment. "Thelma, He loves you so much. Receive His love. Receive Him. Let Him into your heart and life now. Trust Him."

"But I've been so stubborn…for so long."

"Doesn't matter, He sent you the shawl."

"Could you tell me how to…"

Right in the middle of that sentence an orderly pushed her back to her room. She looked over her shoulder at me and mouthed a thank-you. I wanted to run after her, but Jerry was coming out of cobalt, walking very unstably and looking for me.

The weeks crept by. Each day the same. The agony never left. We continued with the radiation treatments, but didn't see Thelma again. Waiting each day, I wanted to see her. It would take only a few minutes to run up to her floor. Jerry offered to go with me. I knew the floor so well. Even where her room was. I could see the floor in my mind. Smell it. Hear the sounds. But I could not go back on that floor. Not yet. Jerry had been hospitalized there several times. The long, shiny hall didn't hold good memories for me. I couldn't even face the ride on the all-too-familiar elevator.

I needed to hear from Thelma. I knew that one of my dear friends worked on Thelma's floor. In fact, I found out that she was caring for Thelma daily. I learned that Thelma had been far from a model patient, but one day she showed up on the floor wearing a beautiful shawl and insisting that it wasn't a shawl at all...but the loving arms of God. And that He loved her! She told her family and strangers about God's love. Thelma insisted that some strange woman had given her the shawl. I thought that perhaps people were beginning to think Thelma was strange, but from what I knew about her, it didn't bother Thelma what people thought. The reports were that she was never without the shawl.

I sent her a copy of a book I had written. Inside I wrote: "Stubborn old women are God's specialty. He loves you. So do I." An avid reader, she devoured the book in a few hours. She began greeting people. Even smiling. Though she became worse physically, her attitude brightened daily. "As sick as she is," my nurse friend said, "Thelma's eyes have a new sparkle."

Little bits of new faith laced with joy insisted upon taking residence in my heavy heart when I thought about Thelma. She reminded me of the absolute truth of Luke 6:38 NASB: "Give, and it will be given to you. They will pour into your lap a good measure—pressed down, shaken together, and running over. For by your standard of measure it will be measured to you in return."

To me it simply meant that whatever you need desperately, you must give away. It sounds foolish, but it works. Even if your husband has a malignant brain tumor, if you need money, you give it away. If you need love, you give that away. And in my case, I needed tremendous faith, so I had to give away what little I had.

God began pouring the faith back into me in an unmistakable way. I saw myself back in that ocean scene knocked over by giant waves. I was under the water, struggling, unable to breathe. But the scene changed in an amazing way.

I was standing. The waves were pounding me viciously, shaking me, trying to knock me down again and again. But I stood like a small rock, almost without effort. And I knew that if I'd never obeyed God and reached out to unlikely Thelma, then I might never have stood in the ocean vision or in real life. But I knew for certain now, from seeing myself stand with those giant waves washing over me, that I was going to stand no matter what came against me. Not in my strength, of course. I had none left. But in God's.

Thelma died in January, wrapped in the soft shawl...and in the arms of the God she had come to know. She learned a lot about how to give out of her need in the short time she had left. My friend who nursed her told me that Thelma decided to leave her sparkling blue eyes to a blind person...someone she'd never met.

THE LONG ROAD BACK

by Evelyn Walker

———⁓———

When I first heard the loud boom outside our house that rainy November day, I thought that a jet had broken the sound barrier. I glanced through the living room window and gasped at the sight of my sixteen-year-old son Timothy sprawled in the street. It was a sight that would change my life.

Just a few minutes before, I'd peeked through that same window after I'd heard Tim's car pull up. He'd been standing and talking with the driver of a red car stopped nearby. I'd stepped back, not letting myself stare, even though I was eager to catch a glimpse of Tim's new girlfriend. He'd driven off earlier to pick her up. Christine Hitchcock, he'd said her name was.

"You'll like her, Mom!" he'd said.

Now I raced out the door, thinking, *He's been run over....*

A girl darted toward me. "Watch out!" she yelled. Behind her, a blond boy lifted a rifle and fired. The girl fell. The boy fired at her again, then swung the gun toward me.

I dove behind my big green Plymouth. The boy charged forward, firing at me at an angle through the car windows. Pain exploded in my abdomen. When I began screaming, the boy jumped into the red car and roared off. My screams brought the neighbors, who phoned for an ambulance and the police.

Everything from then on is a blur. I remember being cold...struggling to answer the questions of the police, but not being able to get my thoughts together...finally sinking into darkness....

I awoke several days later in Albuquerque's Presbyterian Hospital. To save me, surgeons had been forced to do a colostomy. My husband Truman told me then, as gently as he could, that both Timothy and Christine were dead. And already buried.

The pain that hit me then was ten times worse than the agony I'd felt when shrapnel from our bullet-pierced Plymouth had ripped into my stomach.

Tim. My "miracle baby," the son I'd finally managed to keep after miscarrying two other boys. Truman and I had been delirious with joy when Tim had arrived. We already had a sweet little daughter named Cindy, but we'd wanted a boy, too. Cindy and Tim—and then Steve, born two-and-a-half years later. Three beautiful children. Now only two...

When a police detective arrived with photographs of several blond young men, I pointed immediately to one unforgettable face and announced bitterly, "There—that's the boy who shot us!"

The detective told me I had selected an eighteen-year-old college student who was Christine's exboyfriend.

Until that day, the doctors had thought I still might die. From then on I began fighting desperately to get better so I could testify at the trial. Anger burned through me like a dark fire, filling me with an energy that amazed the doctors. I hated the awful thing that had been done to my son.

And I hated God.

Several months before the shooting, Tim had accepted Christ into his life through the influence of one of his friends. Tim had always been a thoughtful, loving son, but after that he became even more considerate. He really cared about how other people felt. But when he'd try to get me to go to church with him, I often made excuses to stay home. Sometimes I would attend a small drive-in church in Albuquerque where I could listen to a sermon without leaving my car. But I'd never had a personal experience with God, so I didn't understand Tim's obvious joy. All I knew now was that Tim had loved God—and God had let him down.

When Nina Green, the wife of the minister of that drive-in church, came to see me in the hospital, I greeted her prayers with cynicism. Yes, I believed in God, I told her. No, I did not believe that God gave much thought about me or anybody else. Certainly not Tim, lying cold and alone in his grave.

"Tim's beautiful spirit is not in that grave!" Nina replied earnestly. "Evelyn, God loves you so much. He's preparing a home for you with Him and with Tim. Tim isn't dead, he's alive, with God."

How could she say a stupid thing like that? I wondered bitterly. I knew where Tim was. He was buried in Sunset Memorial Park in Albuquerque.

I did make it to court to testify, and I heard the boy who murdered Tim and Christine sentenced to two consecutive life terms. I'd expected to feel relief after that. Instead, despair closed in around me like cold fog. I began blaming myself for the murders. Maybe if I'd been more attentive to my family, maybe if I'd gone to church with Tim when he'd asked....

Nina kept in constant contact to assure me that she and others were praying daily that I find peace of mind through the love of Christ. I told her not to bother. Praying couldn't bring Tim back. He was gone. Gone forever.

My husband and our other two children tried to comfort me, but nothing helped. A group from the phone company where my husband worked took up a collection to help pay some of our bills, and they also gave us a white Bible inscribed with Tim's name. I wouldn't read it. When I was home alone during the day, I railed at God out loud.

"I hate You!" I would shout. I'd pick up things and throw them. In my mind, I was throwing them at God.

The doctors who had pieced my body back together now prescribed Valium to calm me down. I took all they recommended—and more. Anything to dull my thoughts. I took Valium with wine to muffle the screaming voices in my head. From then on, I moved through each day in a haze, no longer trying to cook or clean. Truman would often come home from work to find me bombed out of my mind. A couple of times he had to rush me to the hospital to have my stomach pumped.

In desperation he begged me to see a psychiatrist. The psychiatrist I went to did the best he could by having me talk about my anger, but he couldn't give me the one thing I needed—he couldn't give me hope that I'd see Tim again.

My life grew unbearable. One afternoon when I was drunk, I drove very slowly to the cemetery so I could die near Tim. I brought all my pills and a full bottle of wine.

But when I knelt in the grass beside Tim's grave, Nina Green's words came back to me: "Evelyn, God loves you so much. He's preparing a home for you with Him and with Tim...."

Could that be true? But if it were...would a suicide go to heaven? What if Tim really was there, and I did this...?

My thoughts drifted back and forth. There was just enough doubt about it to take me to my car and send me home.

And so it went, for more than two horrible years. All during that time, Nina continued to call to say that people were praying for me. Often I said rude things to her in return. She always responded gently and with love.

Finally, I asked that she leave me alone. I told her emphatically that I wanted nothing to do with God or her.

She replied, "All right, Evelyn, I'll honor your wishes that I not call. But I want you to know that

I will not stop praying for you. God does love you. When you accept Him into your life, you'll find the peace you're looking for."

I did not hear from her again for many months. My rebellion against God and life carried me ever deeper into darkness. I stopped eating almost completely. My weight dropped to eighty-seven pounds.

Ten years after that fateful day, the phone company transferred Truman to an office in Phoenix. When we packed our books for the move, I threw all our Bibles into the trash. Except for one—the white Bible with Tim's name inside. I couldn't bear to toss that one out. In our new apartment in Phoenix, I placed that Bible on the table between the living room and kitchen. Since I could no longer visit Tim's grave, I wanted something that would remind me daily of my lost son.

Truman desperately wanted us to start a new life. He begged me to stop drinking and taking drugs. I did try to cut down, but I found it impossible to quit.

Then came a day in September when I paced the floor, fighting to keep from taking a drink. My mouth burned, my hands trembled. A creaking snap in one of the walls made me start with fear. Was that a gunshot?

"Tim, Tim—" I screamed.

I grabbed the Bible, clutching it to my chest and yelling, "I can't stand it, I can't stand it! God, please! Take away this pain, or let me die!"

I listened in amazement to those words echoing around the room. Was I really asking God for help? I sank down on the couch and opened the Bible with hands that shook so badly I could hardly turn the pages. Near the front I came to a section called "For the Bereaved." I began reading the verses printed there. One in particular leaped out at me from the page: "Let not your heart be troubled: ye believe in God, believe also in me. In my Father's house are many mansions: if it were not so, I would have told you. I go to prepare a place for you" (John 14:1–2 KJV).

That's what Nina had told me!

I read the next selection: "And God shall wipe away all tears from their eyes; and there shall be no more death, neither sorrow, nor crying, neither shall there be any more pain: for the former things are passed away" (Revelation 21:4 KJV).

Upon reading those words, a weight lifted from my body. It's hard to describe what happened next. All I can say is that the darkness fell away as light poured in. Eagerly, I read another verse: "For God so loved the world, that he gave his only begotten Son, that whosoever believeth in him should not perish, but have everlasting life" (John 3:16 KJV).

Tim loved God, believed in Christ...

With the suddenness of a lightning bolt, I knew that Tim was alive! He was alive and with God!

Right then I bowed my head and turned all my problems—the drugs, the fear, the anger—over to the Lord. I asked Jesus to come into my heart.

And He did. Peace flowed into that room like a benediction. I rose to my feet and looked out the window, smiling at the beautiful world I saw there—sunshine, blowing palm trees....

When Truman came home from work, I met him joyfully. "You don't have to worry anymore," I told him. "I'm going to be all right."

I stopped the liquor and drugs that very day. I still had to go through the agony of withdrawal, but now I had the help of God's Word. And, of course, the support of my wonderful husband.

Every day it got a little easier. I've been "straight" for more than two years now.

When I called Nina Green in Albuquerque to tell her I'd accepted Christ, she said happily, "Oh, Evelyn, we never stopped praying for you."

Three years she and others had prayed, never giving up, even when they didn't hear from me. Some of those people never met me, yet still they prayed.

Thank God they did. And thank God for those other beautiful people who gave us the white Bible.

Now I know how important it is to keep praying for people in trouble, to keep telling them that you've asked God to watch over them and help them—even when they act as though they aren't listening. They may be hearing more than they're letting you know, more than they themselves recognize.

Look what the prayers of Nina and her friends did for me. They saved my life.

Going God's Way

by Debra Carney

I did not begin to understand how God works in our lives until I lost one of the most precious people in my life and almost lost another.

We were a happy family, Paul and I with our newborn daughter, Erin. Paul and I met at seventeen, and we were married at twenty-two. He was intelligent and talented. He composed beautiful pop ballads and was an accomplished pianist and singer. And then, tragedy struck us.

On that terrible day, I was wheeling Erin in her carriage through a department store when I noticed that she had turned her head into the pillow. I turned her over. Her face was ashen.

In numbed shock, I was only dimly aware of the relentless sirens, a paramedic holding Erin in a speeding ambulance, the hospital, doctors, Paul rushing into the emergency room gasping, "Deb, where is she?"

For twenty-four hours doctors tried to get some life into her little body. Paul picked up her tiny hand. "It's like ice," he moaned. "She's gone." Erin had died of an illness doctors do not understand. They call it Sudden Infant Death Syndrome (SIDS). She had lived for forty-two days.

Now I became more and more dependent upon Paul. But he was working harder than ever, writing more music, starting his own band. Paul had always been given to sudden emotional impulses that took him off into corners where I couldn't reach him. I had always attributed this to his sensitive, creative nature and had tried to understand. Yet now, when I needed him so desperately, he seemed far away from me. And then he began to drink.

Paul's mother, Jean, a loving, compassionate woman, shared our pain. And she could see what was happening to us. One day she quietly suggested that Paul and I join her at a Thursday night prayer meeting at the Episcopal church that she attended in Saybrook, Connecticut.

"What good will it do?" Paul asked sarcastically. "It's not for me. Besides, I'm too busy."

I, too, doubted that it would do much good.

God—religion—meant even less to me than it did to Paul, who was raised in a strong Christian home, but I appreciated his mother's concern and went along.

That night at the prayer meeting, as I half listened to what was going on, I gradually sensed that I was doing something very peculiar, something I neither initiated nor seemed to control, I was whispering words—the same six words—over and over, "God, please give me another child." I couldn't stop. I clapped my hands over my mouth. Tears began to roll down my face. By the time the meeting ended, I was exhausted and bewildered.

Then, two months later, I became pregnant. I took this as a sign that God had heard my involuntary plea. For the first time since Erin's death, I was heartened. Now I began to attend the prayer meetings regularly. One of my constant prayers was that our second child bring Paul and me closer.

One night Paul came home and told me, "I don't love you anymore." A few days later he packed his clothes and left.

By now my life seemed a shambles. More and more, the prayer meetings at church became my refuge and it was there one night, while praying for Paul and our unborn child, that I felt a stirring within me and heard myself saying aloud, "Lord Jesus, come into my heart." My body felt light, as though it were floating above the ground. At that moment I knew that God was in me, that I had made a total commitment to Jesus Christ.

The next morning I awoke early, feeling as if I were reborn by the rising sun. I yearned to share this happy and wonderful thing with my unhappy husband, but Paul was off, I didn't know where. I prayed for him.

In the months that followed, word came that Paul had become involved with a young woman. I spent the last months of my second pregnancy alone. The days were empty and long, the nights longer and sleepless. My only comfort was in attending church with Jean, who knew how forsaken I felt.

On November 30, though, Paul drove me to the hospital and was there when Shaine was born. He came to visit us once again, but then Shaine and I didn't see him for a while, not even on the day before Christmas when we spent the evening with his parents.

But on Christmas night, my doorbell rang. Not surprisingly, there on the steps stood my in-laws. But standing nervously behind them stood Paul. I welcomed them. Paul's face was pale, his eyes unhappy. Finally, he took me aside. "Deb," he said, struggling to find words, "I'm getting some counseling." For a long minute he looked at me, his blue eyes seemed to be pleading.

For the next few weeks he came to visit, and we talked about our future. "Deb," Paul asked one day, "I want to come home again; may I, please?"

I found myself in a dilemma. I wanted Shaine to grow up in a home with both her father and mother. And I still loved Paul, who was obviously suffering. Finally, I agreed. But when Paul returned home, our struggles were far from over. A restlessness still gnawed at him; he was jittery, distracted, still drinking. Whenever I suggested that we pray or read the Bible or go to a prayer meeting, he shook his head.

"Paul," I begged, "we both need a new knowledge deeper than human understanding, Someone stronger than human strength. We need Jesus Christ."

He looked at me intently. "You've found your way down that road, Debbie," he said, "but it's not for me." He paused. "Yes, I believe in Christ," he added. "But at this point He isn't very much part of my life, is He?" I could almost feel the pain in his eyes.

"Please, Paul," I said, "please come to church with me."

His face flamed. He rose and stalked away, shouting over his shoulder, "Why do you keep trying to drag me to prayer meetings all the time?"

In despair, I turned to Paul's mother for solace. One afternoon after she let me sob my heart out, she said, "Are you sure you're placing Paul in God's hands? Remember when you prayed for another child? God heard you."

Then she leaned forward. "One thing I do know; Paul is like many men. Even when he was a little boy, he was stubborn. The more we tried to push him, the more stubborn he became." She touched my arm. "Why don't you give him up to God?"

I knew deep down she was right. No one can follow another person's path to Christ. Each of us has to find his own way.

And from then on, I relinquished him to God. For a whole year I began all my prayers with, "Lord, enter Paul's heart as You came into mine. I will help in any way You choose." Life was more peaceful after that, but Paul was still suffering.

Then a visiting clergyman from England, the Reverend Trevor Deering, came to our church. I thought Paul might be interested in hearing a speaker from another part of the world. But when I told Paul about Father Deering, I could see the old fire rise in his eyes and I quickly backed off.

However, on the following Sunday, as I was

leaving for church, Paul stopped me at the door. "I'll go with you," he said, adding quickly, "but just this once."

I was elated, but hid my feelings. Once in church I could sense his resistance to everything taking place. He sat there stiff, scowling, silent when the hymns were sung. He heard the call to the altar, watched people answer it. Then, to my amazement, Paul rose slowly and moved down the aisle. "Oh, Lord, he needs Your help," I prayed. But when the clergyman placed his hands on Paul's head, he just stiffly stood there, turned, and hurried back to my side.

On the way home he was silent for a time, then quietly said, "I walked down the aisle because I wanted to cleanse myself of all the wrong I did and the hurt I gave you. But when Father Deering put his hands on my head, I was skeptical that anything could happen. Deb, I just couldn't open my heart."

I prayed for the right words to say. "Will...will you come with me again?" I ventured.

"Maybe. I don't know." And then he added almost under his breath, "I've watched you over the past year, Deb, and you've become so sure, so serene. I wish I could feel the way you do."

The following Sunday night, Paul decided on his own to attend the prayer meeting. In church, Father

Deering and his wife Ann were at the altar. When Father Deering began talking, Paul listened intently. He hunched forward when Father Deering talked of "our inner prison, a prison of our own making. We all want to escape it, but even the most powerful cannot escape it alone. There is only One who can give us the key." Then he invited everyone who had not yet met Jesus to come and meet Him.

Paul stood up. His face was pale, his eyes shining; his fingers gripped my arm. "Deb, come with me," he said softly. I rose and he placed me in front of him, still holding my arm. We followed the first few people down the aisle. At the altar he stood behind me. I heard a noise. I turned. Paul lay on the floor. People were praying over him. Then he got up slowly and led me back to our seats. He was all right, but I was mystified as to what had happened to him.

When the meeting was over, Paul hurried both of us outside. "I wasn't sure anything would happen," he said, his face flushed, his speech rapid, as though he wanted to tell it all at once.

"But when Mrs. Deering put her hands on my head, I felt a surge of peace sweep through me like a big ocean wave. All of my strength left me. Next thing I knew I was on my back, looking up at a ring of faces praying. My mind cleared and I knew I had surrendered myself to the presence of God."

Paul's face was filled with a new light. He looked serene, at peace. He crushed me to him and said huskily, "Deb, I felt as if I were resting in the hands of the Lord!"

"You were, Paul," I said joyously. "You are!"

Since that day, God's hand has been on Paul. His inner turmoil is gone. Of course, our problems didn't all disappear, nor did our marriage become all sweetness and light. But now the two of us are working on them together.

My most important lesson was learning that neither I nor anyone else could determine Paul's salvation. Only God could do that. I could only pray that He would reach a loved one who had wandered away from Him.

Together, Paul and I have found a knowledge deeper than human understanding, and Someone stronger than any human strength.

MIRACULOUS ENCOUNTER

by April Grube

————⁓∭⁓————

I settled into my seat on the red-eye from LA to DC—a trip east to tour some college campuses before I had to make the big decision. The seat next to mine was empty and I couldn't wait to get some sleep. Then I spotted a big guy maneuvering down the aisle, bumping passengers and apologizing profusely, and I knew—lucky me—I had a seatmate. Sure enough, he sat next to me and started talking. "Never did like flying, always too hot or cold. And these seats are too small, don't ya think? But I can't complain. Lord knows, I'm a blessed man...."

So much for sleep. At least I was used to the annoyances of flying. Every summer for the past six years I'd flown to South America for mission trips. I'd heard babies crying nonstop, had my seat kicked and my tray table bumped, often when I was deep in thought or prayer, trying to make sense of my faith in the context of all the suffering I'd seen. Once I'd even lost my favorite book in the mad rush to disembark. So I smiled politely, listening to him chatter away. "Name's Billy," he finally said. "What's yours?"

"April," I said. "April Grube."

Abruptly, the man stopped talking. The strangest look came over his face. "Excuse me, but I didn't quite catch that," he said. I said my name again.

"Have you ever been to South America?" he asked. "When? What airline?" South America? Was he on one of my mission trips? "You don't know me," he said, "but if it weren't for you, I don't know what would've become of me."

Three years earlier, Billy said, he was unemployed, living with his parents, desperately unhappy. He'd gone to South America, hoping new places would renew him. But everywhere he went, he saw suffering. No God would allow such pain, he thought. He headed home more miserable than ever. On the plane back, he searched his seat pocket for headphones. Instead, he found a book, *Searching for God Knows What*, by Donald Miller.

The pages were filled with handwritten notes. At first, Billy said, he laughed at their sincerity and naïveté. But the doubts and questions and thoughts echoed his own. *Here was someone else struggling with their faith*, he thought. He read the book cover to cover. Written on the last page, was the name of the owner: April Grube.

Better Things

by Lisa Coburn

Cigarette smoke hung in the air around me. The club door opened, letting in a breeze from the street. A customer stepped inside. Just another man in a dark suit and tie. Traveling on business, no doubt. Graying hair at his temples gave him a distinguished air, but surely he was the same as all the rest.

I leaned against the wall, avoiding the dirty mirror inches away. I didn't like to see myself dressed as an exotic dancer. Around the club, men sipped overpriced drinks, chatted up the girls, applauded the dancer onstage. I felt cold, familiar anger inside me—men were all the same. Any one of them would take advantage of me if he could. I'd learned that the hard way.

At seventeen, I'd accepted a ride home from college with an acquaintance. The drive turned into a nightmare when he forced himself on me. "Don't even think about telling anyone," he threatened. "I'll kill your family."

I didn't tell a soul. Not even my closest friends. I tried to go on with my life, but I felt like a fake. I looked like any normal student on the outside, but inside I felt dirty and worthless. I dropped out of school. Friends and family were confused by my decision, so it seemed more important than ever to pretend I was the girl I always was. I dated a nice guy named Danny and thought I'd found my salvation when he proposed. I vowed to be the perfect wife. That would take away my shame.

But marriage didn't change a thing. How long could I keep up this charade? I was only pretending to be a respectable wife. If my husband knew the truth about me, he would leave me in a heartbeat. So I left him first.

A few months after Danny and I separated, I ran into an old classmate. "You won't believe what I'm doing," she said. "Exotic dancing at a gentlemen's club."

"How can you stand it?" I asked.

My friend shrugged. "It's no big deal. I dance in

a skimpy outfit and flirt. The pay's not bad either," she said.

A place like that is where you belong, I told myself. *It's all you're good for.*

And there I was. Working in a club, hating myself as much as the men there. I kept my job a secret from Danny. One more dirty secret to add to the list.

The new customer sat down at a table. I adjusted my spaghetti straps and walked over to him. "Join you for a drink?" I asked mechanically.

"Sure," he said. "My name's James." James surprised me by ordering two plain sodas from the bar.

"So, what brings you to West Virginia?" I asked, not caring.

"I'm on assignment." I waited, but he didn't say any more. Instead he asked about me, what I wanted out of life. He talked as if I were a respectable person—which only made me more aware of my revealing costume. *Can't he see what I am?* I wondered.

"I'm due backstage," I said, getting up from my chair.

James stood up, too, and looked into my eyes. "Young lady," he said, "you were created for better things. God loves you. He can turn your life into something beautiful even now."

It seemed as if this man knew my secret, knew what had happened to me. But how could he? "I have to go…." I mumbled, completely shaken.

Backstage, I thought about what James had said. Could things really be different for me? By the time I went back to James's table he was gone. The girls, the bouncers, the bartenders—nobody remembered seeing the distinguished-looking customer.

After that encounter, I could no longer stomach my job. I quit the club and reenrolled at school. I'd have that better life. But this time it wouldn't be pretend. That meant I had to be honest— with myself and the people who cared about me. I would start with Danny. He deserved to know the truth.

Danny seemed skeptical as I settled into a chair across from him at his place. I took a deep breath. "There are things I should have told you before now…. "

Somehow I got it all out.

Danny looked hurt. But I could see he was hurting for me. "Now I understand why you couldn't give our relationship a fair chance," he said gently.

Danny wanted to try again. We got back together.

Or maybe I should say that for the first time, we tru-ly got together. I'd tried so hard to hide. But James showed me I didn't have to go to all that trouble. God knew my secrets and still loved me. Once I felt secure in His love, I accepted my husband's love, too. And finally, after so long, I began to love myself again. I wonder if that wasn't the real assignment that brought James to West Virginia.

3

REASSURANCE
FROM HEAVEN

For I am persuaded, that neither death, nor life,
nor angels, nor principalities, nor powers, nor
things present, nor things to come, nor height,
nor depth, nor any other creature, shall be able to
separate us from the love of God, which is in Christ
Jesus our Lord.

ROMANS 8:38–39 KJV

———————————

*Lord, reassure our hearts with the truth
that nothing can separate us from Your love.*

THE PRAYER
THAT *IS* ALWAYS NEW

from the Editors of Guideposts

—————— ···················· ~m~ ···················· ——————

When I first learned the Lord's Prayer, "heaven," to my young ear, had a faraway sound. It was a remote, fairy-tale kind of place where very good people went after they died. A Father "in heaven" wasn't much help right now!

Since then I've come to feel just the opposite. Heaven, to me, means a reality closer and truer than anything I can see and touch. It means this commonplace earthly life is caught up in God's eternal plan.

The Dutch evangelist Corrie ten Boom had a visual aid that expressed this well. Corrie had arrived for a visit, and my thirteen-year-old daughter

Liz and I were helping her unpack. From the bottom of Corrie's suitcase, Liz lifted a folded cloth with some very amateurish-looking needlework on it. Uneven stitches, mismatched colors, loose threads, snarls.

"What are you making?" Liz asked curiously.

"Oh, that's not mine," Corrie said. "That's the work of the greatest weaver of all." I probably looked as dubious as Liz did.

"But you're seeing it from the wrong side!" Corrie went on. Shaking the cloth open with a flourish, she turned it around to display a magnificent crown embroidered in red, purple, and gold. "You have to look at things from heaven's viewpoint!"

Heaven's viewpoint...when I pray to my Father in heaven, I speak to the One who can make something beautiful of the tangled threads of a lifetime. I am asking Him to help me see the perplexities of daily life "from heaven's side."

Up at Dawn

by Cynthia LaShomb

Some people might think getting up at dawn to do laundry was drudgery. Well, in sultry north central Texas, that was the best time of day to be outside. I enjoyed having those early hours in the fresh air all to myself. It was my favorite time to talk to God and to listen when He talked back to me.

One especially beautiful morning, I pulled my laundry out of the washing machine and headed to the yard. I pinned my clean bed sheets on the clothes-line and praised God. "Your world is even more glorious than usual today, Lord," I said.

A couple of rabbits peeked out of the grass, noses twitching. Two sparrows flew overhead, chasing each other on the breeze. As they disappeared into the distance, their happy whistles were drowned out by another call, this one sad and mournful.

Hee-haw! Hee-haw!

The little donkey who lived down the lane brayed from his lonely field. I heard him most mornings, but each time it broke my heart a little. He had plenty of grass and room to roam, and the breeze was cool and comforting. Still, it made me sad to think of him all by his lonesome in the field.

"God," I said, clipping a pair of socks to the line, "I've got You to talk to. But what about that donkey over there? Who does he have to keep him company in these early morning hours?"

I made no apologies for worrying to God about an animal. From my morning talks with Him, I knew that if a single one of His creatures was unhappy, God felt it. The death of a sparrow meant as much as the death of a king. God would understand my concern. "Please bless that donkey," I asked.

I picked up a towel and straightened it over the line. What was I hearing? I looked behind me and peeked around the hanging towel. The sound was strange, ethereal. Music of some sort. Or singing. Not from a radio, or like any human voice. I felt lifted up by it, as if I might float right off the ground. I stood there mesmerized, and basked in the glorious sound.

"God," I asked, "what is it?" The music faded,

changed tone, and became a more familiar, discordant sound.

Hee-haw! Hee-haw!

It was as if the beautiful, unearthly music I heard had transformed into the donkey's braying. But that was impossible. The two sounds couldn't be less alike, and I would hardly have mistaken one for the other.

Then God spoke to my heart: *"What you heard was the donkey praying to Me, just as he does every day. This morning I allowed you to hear how the donkey's prayers sound to My ears!"*

I went back to work, the donkey's calls drifting over from his field. His braying now seemed joyous. How could any of us ever feel lonely when our God listens and speaks even to the donkey? That morning I was blessed by braying.

MY OLD BIBLE

by Brenda Trimble

························ ——〰—— ························

"A woman in my office recognized your name," my son-in-law, Scott, said to me. He and my daughter, Kim, were visiting me at home. "She can't figure out how. She just said it sounded familiar." Scott told her my name when his friends at the office said they would pray for me. I'd just been diagnosed with an aggressive form of colon cancer. I was only fifty-seven, in good health, with no history of cancer in my family. But now I required surgery, and who knew what else. I was terrified. "Tell her and everyone else I appreciate their prayers," I said. "I need all I can get."

That night I flipped through my Bible, lingering over favorite passages. How many times had a Bible provided comfort in times of fear? I remembered the Bible my husband, Don, gave me on my twenty-seventh birthday, the navy leather cover personalized with my name. I took it to church every Sunday. But one week I left it. I scanned the pews and asked friends if they'd seen it; no one had. I would've kept searching, but soon we moved to another part of Jacksonville and to a new congregation. Not that I regretted the move. We'd been at our current church for over fifteen years, and after my diagnosis, faith, prayers of friends, and of a loving family became my lifeline. Still, even their prayers and the prayers of strangers across town didn't seem like enough to help me.

The next week, Kim and Scott came again. Scott was holding something. "The oddest thing happened," he said. "Remember the woman in my office? It turns out she goes to Englewood Christian." My old church! At once I was flooded with fond memories.

"She knew me there?" I asked.

"No," Scott said. "It was from something she'd seen in a classroom." Then he handed me a well-loved, well-read, navy-colored leather book. And on the cover, in silver lettering, my name.

I've been cancer-free for four years now. I appreciate more than ever my old Bible, which came home to me so unexpectedly when I needed it most.

MY BROTHER CUBBY

by Adam DePrince

It was Christmas week when the New Jersey Division of Youth and Family Services asked my parents to consider the adoption of two preschoolers with hemophilia. As one administrator put it, "You already have so many hemophiliacs, why not two more?"

My mom, my younger brother, Erik, and I had all been born with a rare bleeding disorder, the control of which required transfusions of a frozen, concentrated blood product. My parents had also adopted Mikey, a baby with a severe case of classic hemophilia. He required frequent infusions of a different blood product. Intravenous equipment and syringes were as common around our house as forks and spoons in any ordinary household. What difference would two more beds and a few more cases of clotting factor make?

To be fair to the entire family, my parents felt that we should all be in agreement about these new adoptions. I had always enjoyed my role as a big brother, and I looked forward to the coming of our newest family members, Cubby and Teddy.

I have chosen to tell the story of Cubby, my youngest brother, whose real name is Charles, because it is through him that I have learned to place my trust in God.

Cubby is truly a funny child. He is just naturally that way. He is also naturally loving and trusting. My funny and poignant experiences with Cubby are what I will store away in my memories of him.

A couple of days after he was placed with us, I asked four-year-old Cubby to get dressed so that he could help me shovel the snow off the driveway. Proud that a teenager had asked for his help, he scurried off to get changed.

He came downstairs dressed in a T-shirt and shorts, convinced that shorts were proper attire for the weather. He was bewildered when I explained that it was cold outside. He insisted that it was warm. I scooped him up in my arms and carried him to the front steps in order to end his confusion.

It was plain to see by the astonished look on his face that Cubby had not experienced central heating in his early years.

The fact that Cubby was brown—actually very brown—and we were white was a positive issue in our family. We told him that he was as brown and handsome as a little bear cub. This pleased him immensely.

It was this outlook that led to a hilarious misunderstanding during a camping trip in Maine when Cubby was five. While in the public bathroom of a campground, he struck up a conversation with another camper. The elderly camper asked Cubby if he liked sleeping on the ground. Somehow Cubby thought the man had asked, "Do you like being brown?" "Oh, yes," Cubby replied, "I like being brown." Perplexed, the gentleman repeated his question. Cubby repeated his answer. I decided that these two were never going to close the communication gap and whisked Cubby out the door while he was cheerfully affirming his pleasure over his complexion.

The following summer, while on a backpacking trip, Cubby was concerned about the fact that I had to carry so much more than he. Without warning he decided to help me carry my seventy-pound pack down a trail. I had stopped for a drink from my canteen when Cubby caught hold of the frame of my pack and proudly headed down the slope. The pack weighed thirty pounds more than Cubby, so it dragged him down the path and nearly over a cliff as I frantically chased after him.

Last fall I went for a walk with Cubby and our dog, Stripe. Because of the incline of the hill near our home I had to help Cubby along by pushing his scooter from behind. As I was struggling with the scooter I began to feel bad that I had not noticed before that its wheels were very tight. Cubby wears a full leg brace due to the ravages of hemorrhages in his knee joint. I wondered how he was able to ride the scooter around. At the top of the long, exhausting hill Cubby turned to me and said, "Adam, I was afraid that you might let the scooter roll backward, so I held the brake all the way up to help you."

Now that Cubby's condition is worsening, death is an issue he must confront. He knows that he has AIDS. To avoid the topic would be cruel. He has told me that he is glad that we told him the truth. Now he has time to plan what he wants to do with his very short life. He is also pleased that he can prepare to face death without being "in a panic" on his deathbed.

Death is impossible to deal with if there is no God. Without God, death is not only terrifying for the person dying, but it also creates an unfillable void in the lives of those left behind.

While I was on a walk with Cubby one day, he began asking me questions about heaven. I was deeply touched that this nine-year-old would put so much trust in me. As much as I preferred not to discuss death, I knew I could not let my brother down. I explained to him that life does not end with death. Passing on to heaven is just another, better, part of life. If we are not afraid of being born, then we should not be afraid of dying. I told Cubby that in heaven there is no suffering and that we live with God.

Cubby was comforted to know that there is no hemophilia, crippled legs, or AIDS in heaven. But he was still concerned about missing his family. I reminded him that if there was no suffering, then how could there be homesickness? We decided that time must be different in heaven. It must pass more quickly than on earth. That would definitely explain the lack of homesickness, wouldn't it?

Well, at eighteen I wasn't not much of a theologian, or a child psychiatrist, so I must admit that I agreed with my brother that pizza and the

Teenage Mutant Ninja Turtles would surely be found in heaven. I also promised him that his permanently straight leg would bend in heaven, thus enabling him to fulfill his dream of riding a bicycle.

Cubby was worried that there would be a wait to get into heaven, such as there is at Disney World in December. I assured him that there would never be a line for heaven.

FRESH FROM HEAVEN

from the Editors of Guideposts

--------------------------------- ————⚊———— ---------------------------------

*I*n heaven," says my four-year-old son, with the confidence of a man talking about his native country, "everyone is one hundred inches tall." He goes on at some length about the geography and nature of heaven, what sort of boots people wear there (red ones), what the angels do all day long (play basketball), even what's for breakfast (cookies).

These pronouncements draw guffaws and scorn from his brother and sister, but he holds forth with undiminished verve. "Yeah, I remember that heaven," he says, with affection. "God was there all the time. He's a really big guy. He laughs all the time. He's a funny guy. He has really big hands. He's bigger than Daddy. I was not scared because He was laughing."

More scorn from his siblings and a grin from his mother, but his father is moved to ruminate on the topography of heaven, and not for the first time, either. Did not this boy come from God? Didn't his long-legged sister and his exuberant brother also come from God? And the lovely woman sipping coffee and smiling across the table? And the air we all breathe and the vast country outside and the crow on the fence cocking a curious eye at the heavenly boy in the house? None would be but for the Maker. And who is to say that this boy does not remember a place he was a mere four years ago?

So I listen with care and hear of a country filled with joy and peace and light and laughter. Many days I think that I am in heaven right now, right here, in the sea of love that is my family. But listening to the little prophet at the head of the table, I dream for a moment of the world to come, the world we work toward, the place God has prepared for us.

BESIDE STILL WATERS

by Betsy Young

───∿───

$\mathcal{M}$y husband was gravely ill. In desperation, his doctors prescribed bypass heart surgery, a new and untested procedure at the time. Bob and I were both frightened and needed a reprieve. A week before his surgery, we packed a picnic and on a glorious California day drove out to the Mojave Desert.

Bob loved the desert air, it was so dry and easy to breathe. We traveled aimlessly on back roads lined with desert flowers, yucca and the lovely paloverde tree. And then, on an off-road track, we chanced upon a path. We left the car, and the path led us to a gentle stream of water. Such streams aren't unheard of in the Mojave in June, but they're rare.

We sat beside a shaded pool and over the next few hours—picnicking, sunning—we were as happy as we'd ever been during our twenty-five years of marriage. The water, so unexpected, so soothing as we soaked our feet, especially pleased Bob. "The Lord leadeth us beside the still waters," he said to me. And indeed, as we talked, the waters seemed to wash away our fears. Our souls were restored.

Reluctantly we left. But back at the car, Bob realized he'd left his knife on a poolside stone and I walked back to retrieve it. There was the knife, glinting in the sun. But the brook...the pool...they were gone. Where there had been water minutes earlier, there were now only stones and sand.

The following week, Bob died on the operating table, his heart condition even worse than the doctors had suspected. I'm sure, though, that he died in peace, assured by our stream that he would dwell in the house of the Lord forever.

GLIMPSE OF PARADISE

by Audre L. Tribbe

⸺⧟⸺

Springtime in Washington, cherry-blossom time. When that wonderful sea of pink blossoms foams along our capital's avenues, I always wish everyone in the world could see it. So one year, I invited my parents to come down from Cape May, New Jersey, to visit me at cherry-blossom time. Word came back, however, that health problems made such a trip impossible. Then, on the very day when I had hoped they could be with me, I received a telephone call at the office telling me that my mother had just died.

I sat there stunned with disbelief and shock. Finally, I organized my office work after a fashion, told my coworkers that I would be gone for a week, and walked down the stairs at the US Naval Oceanographic Office. As I reached the street, I was trembling, overwhelmed by the terrible sense of grief and loss. Somehow I made my way to my car and put my keys in the ignition. And as I did, I heard Mother's voice say quite clearly and distinctly, "Oh, Audre, if you think the cherry blossoms are beautiful, you should see what I'm seeing!"

Then I cried, but in joy as well as sorrow.

A Glowing Cross

by Bill Dolack

———ﾊﾉ———

My dad was in the hospital battling an intestinal infection when his vital signs plummeted and he was rushed to the operating room. After a hurried consultation with Dad's doctors, Mother braced my sister and me for the worst.

Throughout my childhood, my father had survived a number of serious medical problems, including a heart attack and cancer. He'd seen the four walls of a hospital room more times than anyone should have to. *Lord,* I prayed, *no matter what, please comfort him.*

Dad pulled through. As soon as he felt better he told us something amazing about that day in the operating room.

"I was scared. I knew I was dying," he said. "I shifted my head to one side and watched the nurses prepping for the operation. Beyond them I saw a large window. Out in the dusk, was a lighted cross, glowing as if meant for me. I stared out that window, my eyes focused on the brilliant outline. My fears subsided. Then the anesthesia took hold."

Dad recovered fully and several months later went to visit a friend at the same hospital. In the parking lot, Dad looked around for the cross he'd seen through the window. He couldn't find it. Inside he ran into one of the nurses who had taken care of him. "Can I take a quick look at the operating room where I had my surgery?" he asked. The room was free, so she took him in. My father was dumbfounded. There was no window in that room. All four walls were solid through and through.

In My Father's House

by Marion Carmin Aag

───※───

When I was a teenager, I overheard Dad telling my mother, "Of all the passages in the Bible, I think this is my favorite: 'In my Father's house are many mansions: if it were not so, *I would have told you*'" (John 14:2 KJV, emphasis added). In the years since, I have heard that verse many times, but never have I heard anyone put emphasis on the second part as Dad did.

I think that statement meant so much to him because of his tumultuous early life. When he was only twelve, his home broke up due to the stress of family deaths, illness, and poverty. The children were sent to an agency and then farmed out to different homes. The man who took Dad in treated him cruelly. Dad ran away and for years he was homeless, surviving by picking up odd jobs. In his early twenties, he finally settled down. He met and married my mother and together they raised a family. Dad always made sure to give us the happy home he had never had.

When I turned seventeen, I married and moved to the West Coast. Even though I couldn't see Dad often, we stayed in touch through letters and phone calls. Then Dad's health began to decline. He struggled for years with diabetes, arteriosclerosis and Alzheimer's. When my mother could no longer care for him, he had to be admitted to a nursing home.

I was devastated when I received the call telling me Dad had passed away. After explaining to my children what had happened, I went to my bedroom for a while. Lying on my bed, I recalled the little Baptist church that we'd attended in East Delavan, Wisconsin, and the Sunday night when Dad and Mom responded to an old-fashioned altar call. For the next several years, I had watched their faith grow.

Now as I wept for my father, I wondered why his life had been so brief and so difficult even though his faith seemed so deep. Just then my thoughts were interrupted by a sound at the door. I looked over and saw little fingers pushing a sheet of paper through the gap underneath.

I picked up the paper and read the childish printing of my eight-year-old daughter. When I opened the door, I saw her slipping away. "Rachel," I said, "where did you get this?"

"Well, Mommy," she said, "I knew you felt sad about Grandpa, and I asked God to please give me something from the Bible to help you. I opened it up and copied a verse."

On the paper was John 14:2. Then I was comforted, knowing Dad finally was in the heavenly home he had cherished. If it were not so, I would not have been told.

ETERNAL PARTY

from the Editors of Guideposts

—————

"This is not the way I dreamed of spending my Saturday," I mumbled under my breath. My husband Jacob had to work, so here I was doing all the household chores on a beautiful summer weekend. *What I should be doing is swimming at the lake,* I said to myself, pulling off the yellow gloves I wore to do the dishes.

I was feeling pretty sorry for myself and more than a little annoyed as I picked up the bottle of spray bleach and headed into the bathroom. A small voice brought me to an abrupt halt.

"Mommy, what is heaven?"

I looked down at Trace, my four-year-old. He was staring up at me, a serious look in his big gray eyes. I swallowed and knelt down so I could look into his face.

"Well," I said, trying to think of all the correct biblical answers but drawing a blank, "heaven is...." I looked down at the bleach in my hands. "Heaven is...a big party."

"A party?" He looked confused.

"Yes. A big party, where we get to be with God and all the people we love. Remember how much fun you had at Jeremiah's birthday party? Remember the cake and presents and games?" Trace nodded. "Heaven is like that: a big, wonderful party."

A smile spread across his face. "Awesome, Mommy," he said. Then he hugged me and ran off to play.

I returned to my work knowing that had I not been at home doing housework, I would have missed the chance to have such a great conversation with my son. It wasn't such a bad Saturday after all.

4
HEALING FROM HEAVEN

$\mathcal{B}$less the LORD, O my soul; and all that is within me, bless His holy name! Bless the LORD, O my soul, and forget not all His benefits: who forgives all your iniquities, who heals all your diseases, who redeems your life from destruction, who crowns you with lovingkindness and tender mercies.

PSALM 103:1-4 NKJV

Thank You, Lord, for using Your awesome power to heal us.

Look, Mom, It's Gone

by Cheryl Gade

We had moved from Minnesota to Spokane, Washington, after my husband accepted a management position at a craft store. Our first summer was filled with getting our new house in order, finding a school for the boys, and locating a good church.

The bold messages taught by our new pastor caused us to act on our beliefs and be "doers" of the Word (James 1:22). Faith seemed new and fresh to us as we discovered a deeper walk with God.

Bedtime has always been precious to our family. One storybook reading often turned into two or three. After a Bible story, the boys cleverly offered their personal translation of the story by adding unique details. Sweet voices prayed for blessings, hugs and kisses were shared, little bodies were tucked in, and the lights were turned off.

One night, while kissing my youngest cherub, Douglas, I noticed a bubble at the base of his teeth. With the growing experience of raising three rambunctious boys, I did not panic over the unexpected find but decided to keep an eye on the growth that made its home in my son's mouth.

I examined Douglas's mouth nightly. The bubble consistently grew until it caused his lip to protrude. We questioned him with growing concern. "Does it hurt? Can you move it with your tongue? Does it bother you?"

Douglas had developed into a tough little boy by having two older brothers. Though only three, he knew how to handle the rough stuff. Ear infections never bothered him and fever did not slow him down. This new challenge provoked no bother or worry to my young lad. I, on the other hand, was concerned enough to pursue a solution.

Being new to the city, we asked around to locate a trustworthy dentist. After a quick examination, we were ushered into the dentist's office. "I've never seen anything like this before," the doctor said with concern.

We were immediately referred to another dentist who could surgically remove the growth. They planned to anesthetize Douglas, then biopsy the bubble once it was removed.

My thoughts reeled. He's only three, Lord. I don't want him to have surgery. We didn't even have insurance yet. Gathering up my innocent child, who knew nothing of the fear that had descended on his mother, we headed to see his father at work.

My detailed report to Scott was solemn. "Call and schedule the surgery," he offered as a logical conclusion. "We have to get this taken care of." I knew Scott well enough to realize he was equally concerned about Douglas, yet he stood strong to carry me through my weak moment.

Hearing our dilemma, the assistant manager spoke up, "Well, we'll just believe that he'll be fine, in Jesus' name. God will take good care of him!"

We stared at her in wonderment. Faith! I was quickly reminded that faith was more powerful than any sickness or disease that would attempt to place itself on our child.

That night, bedtime was sweet as always. However, after the Bible story, Scott took control of our prayer time. "We're going to pray for Douglas's mouth," he said with authority.

We had learned from the Scripture that if someone was sick, we could lay hands on him and pray in faith for his healing. Douglas's two older brothers bounded out of bed, jumped onto Douglas's bed, and laid their little hands on their brother. Scott placed his hand on his chin and prayed a simple prayer of faith while I stroked his hair. After hugs and kisses, the boys jumped back into their beds, and the lights went out.

The next day was bright and sunny. Waking the boys, I took a few minutes to rub backs and tousle hair. When Douglas welcomed me with a bear hug, I quickly asked him if I could look inside his mouth as I had done each morning for many days.

Douglas dutifully pulled down his lip on one side, revealing a pink, healthy gum line. Hmm, I thought. It must be the other side. He pulled down the lip on the other side. I saw nothing.

"Douglas, open your mouth wide," I commanded. Inspecting his mouth as a buyer would inspect a horse, I found no abrasion, scar, or redness, only clear, pink gum tissue. The ugly looking bubble had completely disappeared. Smothering my baby with hugs as he squirmed to get loose, I celebrated our miracle. Douglas's attention was already focused on breakfast.

The Moose and a Miracle

by Kerry Sprague

.... ⟶⟶⟶ ....

I tossed and turned in bed, trying not to wake my husband Don, who slept peacefully beside me. My heart raced, my palms were sweaty and I could barely breathe. Another panic attack was keeping me awake.

I had struggled with anxiety for nearly twenty years. I had tried everything—counseling, medication, acupuncture; you name it, I had tried it—and nothing helped. I felt worthless as a wife and mother of two girls. I could barely cope each day; much less take care of my family. I prayed as the tears silently trickled down my cheeks, "Lord, please take my life. I can't do this anymore." I was too afraid to take my own life, so instead I begged God to do it. I wiped my tears away with the edge of my comforter.

As I watched the sun rise and brighten the sky, dread filled me. I had to face another day. My husband knew about my anxiety attacks but he had no idea how I longed for my life to end. No one knew that.

I forced myself to get up. I had two little girls who needed to eat, and we were getting ready to go on a two-week road trip to visit the national parks throughout the western United States. Our plan was to start with the nearby Rocky Mountain National Park in Colorado, then visit Wyoming, Montana, Alberta, Idaho, Washington, and back through Wyoming to our home in Boulder, Colorado. I should have felt excited about this vacation, but I just feared the trip. As I packed the girls' bags, I hoped that two weeks away would give me some relief from my anxiety. Maybe I'll see a moose, I thought as I zipped up the last bag. That might bring some joy in my life. I had seen a moose once when I was a little girl and had always wanted to see another one.

The next morning, after another sleepless night, we loaded up our Jeep and buckled the girls into their car seats. I took my spot in the passenger seat, and tried to put on a smile.

"We're off," Don said. "This is going to be a great trip."

"It'll be fun to be away for a couple of weeks," I said. I didn't want to disappoint Don so I pretended to be excited, but inside I was scared. I worried about the car breaking down, where we would stay at night, if the girls would get sick, if the weather would ruin our trip, if Don would have fun. I fought the panic that threatened to smother me.

I did my best to appear cheerful and enjoy the trip, but I continually battled panic attacks. I also kept secretly wishing to see a moose. This became more and more important to me as we covered more miles. I wanted to see one, to remember the joy I'd felt as a child, to know I could have some relief from my anxiety, even if for a moment. This would some-how give me assurance that I could be okay in the future. As we neared the end of our vacation, my hope to see a moose faded. The usual gloom I felt began clouding my thoughts as the rain clouds dark-ened the skies. We entered northern Wyoming in a thick fog, making it difficult to see much, but on the side of the road I noticed a moose crossing sign.

"Okay, girls, you know how we haven't seen a single moose on this whole trip?" I said, looking over my shoulder. They nodded their heads in uni-son "Well, I need you to help me spot one. Can you guys keep your eyes on the lookout for a moose?

This is where we might see one before we get home."

The girls, Don, and I began searching the hillsides, trying desperately to see a moose. This game helped pass the time, but no luck—no moose.

On the last day of our trip, I had given up all hope of seeing one. I fought back the tears that were pooling in my eyes. It was time to go home and continue fighting my unending battle with anxiety. In desperation I silently cried out to God, *Lord, I need to know if I'm going to be okay. Will You please show me a moose? But, Lord, it can't be any moose just walking out of the woods—it has to be something unique. I need to know it's a sign from You that I'll be all right.*

We were only a few hours from home as Don turned into Dubois, a little town in Wyoming, to get gas. As we came around the corner into town I couldn't believe what I was seeing. On my right was a car wash and on the roof of the building stood a giant concrete moose.

"Don, stop! I have to get a picture of that moose," I practically yelled.

"What?" he asked.

"You're not going to believe this, but I just prayed and asked God to show me a moose, a sign from Him to me, but not just a moose off in the distance, but somehow unique, so I would know it was from Him."

"Well, that's definitely unique," he said as he smiled and pulled into the car wash lot.

I grabbed my camera, stood in front of the beast and clicked. *Whirrrr*. "Oh, no, I'm out of film! I have to have a picture of this."

We drove around to a few nearby stores, but it was Sunday and after 5:00 p.m., and all the stores were closed. Yet I still felt excited that God had answered my prayer. We drove home.

Unfortunately, during the next five days, my anxiety drastically increased. I hardly slept or ate anything. Don asked his mom to come over and help with the girls because I could barely function. I thought often about that moose, but as time went on and I became worse, my thoughts turned negative. It wasn't a real moose anyway. Or that probably wasn't from God. I chided myself for holding hope in seeing a silly concrete moose.

Then on the fifth night, I hit rock bottom as I stared at the static on the TV in our family room. "Lord, please either help me or take my life," I pleaded again. I tried to sleep on the couch, but kept watch as the clock slowly ticked toward morning. Around 3:00 a.m., I heard a still, small voice say, *"Look for the cross in the moose picture."*

What moose picture? I didn't get a picture of it. *I'm losing my mind,* I thought as I rolled onto my back. Then I heard it again, *"Look for the cross in the moose picture."* I shook my head. I had to be making this up. Then I heard the same words for a third time. Maybe I wasn't making it up. I decided to take the film in the next day.

The next morning, feeling ridiculous about what I was doing, I prayed, "Lord, if that voice was from You last night, then let me grab the right roll of film." I reached into the brown paper bag that held forty rolls of undeveloped film and grabbed one roll.

I went to the grocery store, dropped off the roll at the one-hour developing counter, and shopped for an hour. When I picked up the film, my hands were shaking. I desperately wanted to see a cross in the picture, but I didn't even know if this was the right roll of film or if I even got that picture of the moose. I opened the envelope right there and flipped through the pictures.

Then I saw it, the moose on top of the car wash. I had captured it on film after all. I stared at it, looking for a cross. My eyes studied the moose, then the clouds in the sky, and suddenly a shiver went through my body. There in the sky were two jet streams crossing over each other—a cross! "Wow! Thank You, Lord," I whispered.

When I got home, I called Don. I told him about the voice I'd heard in the night and the picture. I choked back sobs as I said, "I can't believe God would do this for me. I know I'm going to be okay."

From that moment on, my healing began. For the first time in twenty years I began to see results. I felt purpose in my life. I began doing things I never would have dreamed of doing before, like teaching a Bible study, speaking publicly, and volunteering in my daughters' classrooms. I even slept peacefully and ate normally. Slowly my anxiety disappeared and was replaced with an excitement for life and a peace that was foreign to me.

I still keep the picture of that moose with the cross in it as a reminder that God healed me from my anxiety. But, more importantly I know God answers prayer. He answered mine in a way that had meaning just for me.

Miracle in Mozambique

by Brenda Lange

People thought I was a little crazy to start Village of Love in Mozambique. A single woman running an orphanage by herself in a desperately poor, politically unstable country? But something told me this was my life's calling. I had skills as a nurse, and as a result of decades of civil war, Mozambique was a country of orphans. I knew my path wouldn't be easy, but I had faith that God would give me the direction and strength necessary to do His work.

My first step was to enroll in a school for missionaries in Africa. There I was trained to help the needy by using local labor and materials. I was also taught to respect local customs. The last thing children in a Third World orphanage need is to feel that their language and beliefs are being wrested from them. They have already lost so much.

After graduating in 1992, I set my sights on Majune, an especially impoverished area in the low, hot, northern region of Mozambique. The orphanage would essentially be a one-woman operation, so I needed to find support from some of the locals. That's why I was so thankful to God for sending me my assistant director, Crispo.

Crispo spoke five tribal languages in addition to English and Portuguese. The orphanage opened in 1995, and whether bargaining for a part for our pickup truck, procuring supplies for the orphanage, or negotiating the maze of Mozambique politics, Crispo was the one I counted on daily. Without his skills—and his deep love for the children who kept pouring through our gates—the orphanage would never have made it.

Early one July morning in 1997, Crispo had gone with Janito, a local farm worker, to tend some game traps set along the nearby Lugenda River.

That afternoon I was just beginning to wonder what was taking them so long when I heard Janito shouting breathlessly as he dropped his bicycle.

"Crispo snake bit!"

Seeing Janito's look of panic, I didn't need to ask what kind of snake. The black mamba is the most feared reptile in sub-Saharan Africa. Growing as long as thirteen feet, it can travel as fast as a man can run and delivers one of the world's most lethal bites. Even if the venom itself isn't fatal, a fast-moving infection can prove hazardous.

"We were checking the traps along the river when we surprised the snake," Janito explained. "A big one! It bit Crispo before we could get away."

During my first days in Africa, I'd had a wonderful donkey I christened Old Faithful. One morning I'd awakened to find the poor animal dead. Two ugly marks on his belly suggested the culprit was a mamba. The snake's venom is so powerful that human victims lose the ability to speak within minutes. Suffocation follows as the chest muscles stop working. Crispo could be dead already.

God, I know You always help me, I prayed. *Please help Crispo.* I grabbed the keys to the pickup, and Janito and I raced to the river's edge.

Crispo was sitting upright on a log, staring into space with a glazed expression frozen on his face. Two bright purple marks were clearly visible on the back of his hand. His entire arm was swollen to twice its normal size, and was as hard as a tree trunk.

"Crispo, can you hear me?"

Nothing.

I'm a nurse. I didn't need to have the facts

explained to me. I'd faced just about every problem imaginable in Mozambique: floods, infections, diseases, rebel attacks. Crispo had always been there for me. When others judged something impossible, Crispo said, "We will see, Miss Brenda." Now the man who had single-handedly done so much to make my dream of making the orphanage a reality could soon be gone. There wasn't a thing I could do about it. Nothing.

An idea occurred to me—an idea so outrageous, it could only have come from God. I had to say it out loud just to keep believing it: "Crispo! You are not going to die. Can you hear me? *You are going to live!*"

Mamba antivenin is costly to produce. I knew there wasn't a chance of us being able to find any. But we could at least get Crispo to a clinic. The nearest sizable one was in Lichinga, four hours away on primitive, treacherous roads. On the way we'd pass the village of Malanga, which had a much smaller clinic. Maybe we could pick up some antibiotics there to keep the infection at bay.

I put Crispo right next to me in the pickup, trying my hardest to keep him awake with a steady stream of talk as we lurched down the road.

"Crispo," I said, almost shouting, "I depend on you, and the children do too. You will live. You will not die." And with this thought came renewed faith. As Paul wrote, "In everything give thanks, for this is the will of God."

Lord, thank You for sending Crispo to help me. Thank You for his friendship over these years. Thank You for keeping him alive by the river long enough for me to reach him. Yes, I could be thankful even in this.

Crispo gave no indication that he understood my words. His breathing was labored, but he was still alive. "Breathe, Crispo, breathe!" I finally shouted at him. "You're going to make it."

I jammed on the brakes the second we reached Malanga, pulling up in front of the clinic in a cloud of dust. Crispo stirred. Amazingly, he turned and spoke clearly: "Miss Brenda, I feel better."

I was completely numb with shock. At the very least, Crispo should have been comatose by that time.

Some of the villagers had begun to gather around the truck sensing something was wrong. I couldn't believe my eyes as Crispo opened the passenger door and walked slowly up the stairs of the little clinic. That in itself was a miracle.

I raced inside ahead of Crispo. "My friend was bitten by a black mamba over half an hour ago," I hastily explained to the male nurse on duty. "He needs an antibiotic shot right now."

The man shook his head. "Every drop of our medicine is precious. We can't waste it on a dead man."

Crispo is not going to die! I reminded myself. "No!" I barked like a drill sergeant. "This man is going to live. We're not leaving until you give him that antibiotic." I stared determinedly at the nurse until he relented.

Crispo received his shot, and after refilling our water jug, we got back in the truck for Lichinga.

Evening was coming on—always a dangerous time to be on the road in Mozambique. Not long after we left Malanga, the sun began to set. We came to a long, rickety log bridge spanning a river. Normally we would have made a careful inspection on foot before taking the truck out onto it. Today there was no time for that. Foot by foot, I edged the pickup onto the bridge's crooked, hand-cut slats. The wood groaned beneath our wheels as we crept above the fast-moving water. Finally, the pickup's tires touched solid ground on the far side.

As we bounced along the rutted road, Crispo's lips and fingers began to turn blue. His skin felt dangerously cool, and his breathing became increasingly irregular. An hour passed and then another. Every few minutes I reached over and checked to make sure Crispo was still breathing. *Still alive, still alive.*

In the final hour of the drive, Crispo started to rally more and more. By the time we arrived at the hospital in Lichiga he was fully alert and awake. It was almost 8:00 p.m.—more than four hours since he had been bitten.

The town's generator wasn't working, and the hospital's small emergency room was lit only by a few solar lights. A doctor appeared and quickly examined Crispo's hand. The swelling had all but disappeared in the few hours since we had passed through Malanga.

"I assume this bite just occurred," the doctor said, writing in his chart.

"No, it happened at about three this afternoon," I explained.

"Impossible. If that were so, the arm would be much more swollen....and this man would probably be dead."

With God, nothing is impossible.

"I know it's hard to believe. But I'm a nurse, and I assure you he was bitten over four hours ago."

"Keep him still," the doctor instructed, shaking his head as he left the room. A little while later the doctor returned with another shot of antibiotics.

We spent the night at a nearby mission and managed to make it back to the orphanage by early afternoon the next day. There, we found Crispo's relatives preparing for his funeral. When he stepped out of the truck, I thought all of them were going to faint.

The following morning I went to check on Crispo and found his bed empty.

"He already left for Malanga," Janito told me with a smile. "He said he wanted to see the looks on everyone's faces when they saw a ghost drive up on a motorbike!"

For weeks Crispo was a celebrity. "All I can remember from when I was on the truck was Miss Brenda telling me that I would live," Crispo said. Everybody wanted to see his wounds: the proof of what he had lived through. Our orphans were especially impressed. It was miraculous.

But what is still most amazing to me was that after Crispo was bitten, I hadn't needed proof that he would survive. That was God's gift to me at the moment of my greatest fear. The facts had argued for Crispo's death, and faith had argued against the facts. For those four hours I clung to my faith, and against the odds, Crispo lived.

I have always believed that without Crispo there would be no orphanage called Village of Love. Now I know that God believes it too.

Silent Treatment

by Kathy Mattea

.... —⁄⁄⁄— ....

I had never experienced anything quite like it.
Several years ago, I was performing at a club in
London. Near the end of the set, I was singing
"You're Not the Only One" when I reached for a
high F near the top of my vocal range. What came
out, however, didn't sound like me. I felt like a rock
climber grabbing a familiar handhold only to have it
crumble away.

I got through the final number and an encore,
but as I walked offstage the band gathered around me.
Those guys knew my voice inside out. They could tell
it had been more than a simple missed note.

My manager rushed backstage. "Are you all right?"
he asked, concern tightening his voice.

"I'm fine. Just a little tired." My mind was racing.

All singers have ups and downs. No one is 100 percent every night. You just learn to sing around problems. My schedule was booked tight, and I had obligations to promoters, audiences, my musicians, and crew. To stop would mean more pressure than going on. I couldn't quit. I had been on an award-winning streak for three years, and I had waited all my life for the touring opportunities I now had.

I've loved music ever since I can remember. I was a precocious kid, and early on teachers warned my mom to keep me busy so I wouldn't get bored. She threw me into every activity she could think of, and music was the one thing that stuck. It never bored me; there was always something to learn. I learned piano and guitar, then started singing. Eventually I began playing at our tiny church in Nitro, West Virginia, picking guitar and singing solos. There was something earthy and real in our little church. The music was heartfelt, and everyone sang as loud as they could. My years there taught me that music is a way to embrace God, and I never doubted where my singing came from.

After two years at West Virginia University, studying engineering and physics, I missed music so much I decided to move to Nashville. I had always dreamed of a music career, and I prayed for guidance. I didn't care if I became famous; I was in search of a more interesting life. After some rough months, I began a spiritual ritual of putting myself in God's hands every day. I prayed for a path, a niche, and I prayed for clear vision. If I didn't have what it took, I wanted to be able to let go and get on with my life.

But I found my path, and it had led to the stage in London that night. Exciting things were happening, yet they were coming at me so quickly I didn't have time to enjoy them. I started feeling the pressure of success, the double-edged sword that it can be. Some mornings I woke up more tired than when I went to bed. When I began to question my feelings, the guilt kicked in. Who was I to complain? How many people would like to be exactly where I was now? Didn't I have everything I ever wanted? Hadn't God put me on my path? I began to wonder if I was having a nervous breakdown.

After the London show I flew back to Nashville. At that point I couldn't even sing. The next morning I saw Dr. Ed Stone at the Vanderbilt Voice Clinic.

"Just relax, Kathy," he said as he passed a fiber optic instrument attached to a video camera to the back of my throat. I tried to breathe and stay calm. I looked at a monitor. The camera would show my vocal cords, a pair of membranes no thicker than a nickel that produce a miraculous range of sound.

"Say, 'Aah.' "

"Aah…"

I saw my epiglottis move and then something truly horrifying. I expected my cords to be raw and red, even a bit swollen, par for the course after a long run. But I had never seen anything like that—a large red ball, like a blood blister, directly on top of one of the cords. Instinctively, I pulled back and gasped. Before I could stop myself, I was sobbing.

Doctor Stone let me cry for a while, then softly encouraged me to let him take a closer look. I wiped my tears and tried to compose myself. "Kathy, you need complete vocal rest," he said. "You must not sing. You must not speak, not a word, not even a whisper. Try not to laugh. You need to rest. Not just your voice but your whole body. Take a little time off. Relax."

After three weeks, the doctors at the Voice Clinic would have another look. We would learn more about our options when they could see my cords without the swelling and inflammation. No one said it, but we were all thinking surgery. I had three weeks of nothing to do but worry about the future.

My manager had come to the clinic, and we discussed canceling all my engagements for two months.

He didn't blink an eye. "Done," he said. I drove home and explained the situation to my husband, Jon. That was the last I would talk for twenty-one days.

It was strange taking time off in the middle of summer, usually my heaviest touring season. And it was odder still to be utterly silent. No rehearsals, no meetings, no interviews, no chats with friends. I went from ninety miles an hour to a screeching halt. At first it was uncomfortable, and then I began to feel peaceful. I listened more. I began to realize how much I used my voice to define myself, in all aspects of my life. And I had no choice but to sit quietly, alone with myself even in a crowded room.

That first day, after my conversation with Jon, I laced on an old pair of running shoes and hit the beautiful walking trails of Radnor Lake, a nature preserve six miles from downtown Nashville. I needed to take some action in order to feel I was contributing to the healing process, and that was my first step.

I started going for long walks every day. As I wandered through the sun-dappled woods on the ridge overlooking the lake, I held silent conversations with myself and listened for answers. At first, the walking gave me comfort—the feeling of getting away from my problems. But as time went on, my physical exercise became spiritual exercise. I thought about my priorities.

I thought about the role my work played in my life. I worked hard, and I loved it. Still, I felt overwhelmed by success, and at times my life seemed out of control. Where had I gone wrong? I thought back to simpler times in my life—to West Virginia and our little church. I had found my voice there. It had felt so right to sing. Had I ruined my voice by doing what I thought God wanted me to do? How could I make sense of that? What if I couldn't sing ever again? What if I was never the same? Waves of fear would wash over me, and I'd cry uncontrollably.

But during my walks I began to face fear and regard it as my constant companion. I would visualize it as a small creature that lived on my right shoulder. It looked, in my mind, like a gargoyle. It wasn't going to go away, but I had God on my side. Eventually I became bold enough to talk to it. In my mind I would say, I can't get rid of you, but I am going through this to the other side, and God is going to lead me. I began to realize that I had no idea what God had planned for me. Maybe there was some other path I was supposed to take, and this was His way of getting me there.

I began to see small signs. While waiting for a CAT scan of my neck to check for tumors, I spotted a little girl, about five. She was on her dad's lap, and I could see a catheter tube peeking out from under her gown. I looked around the room at an elderly man on a gurney, waiting as I was. He was pale and thin. And I realized that those people had much bigger struggles than I had. My condition was not life-threatening. I would go on, voice or not. I would find the next thing to do. Suddenly I knew it would be okay, that God was indeed taking care of me, in His own way.

As my daily walks continued, I began to realize it was my soul as much as my body that needed healing. I began to see my injury (my "ruby," as I had come to nickname it) as a gift. Nothing else would have gotten my attention in the same way.

I surrendered myself completely. And I was truly ready for whatever happened next.

The three weeks of silence passed quickly, and after another three weeks of vocal therapy, I cautiously returned to singing. I began to tour again, and even recorded another album. I was living with the injury and doing well, until it hemorrhaged about a year later. Surgery became unavoidable at that point. It was a bit of a roller-coaster ride, but I had new reserves and my physical and spiritual beliefs to get me through it. I just kept turning everything over to God. He was in control—not me, not my fear, and not even my doctors, ultimately.

The surgery was a success and today my voice is stronger than ever. More importantly, my faith is stronger. Like my body, it needs daily exercise. When I do my spiritual calisthenics life doesn't seem so complicated and stressful. Everything certainly does not always happen the way I want it to. I have setbacks and disappointments. I question as much as I accept. But that's how I grow.

Earlier this year I went through some soul-searching. And for one of the few times in my life I asked God for a concrete answer. I sent up a prayer asking for some confirmation that I was offering something with my singing. I said, "If I'm supposed to quit, just let me know. I'll go on to the next thing if it's time...."

That night, while I met fans after the show, a woman was walking away after having her picture taken with me. She stopped, turned around, took hold of my arm, looked me directly in the eye and said, "Don't quit. Your music means so much to us."

It was all I needed to hear.

SOMEONE WATCHING OVER US

by Donna Lowich

———⟋⟍———

*I*t was Saturday and the last day of our family vacation together. We had spent the week at the beach near Atlantic City. It had been a great time for all of us. Somehow we had managed to arrange everyone's schedule so that we could be together. My family unit included my parents, my husband Walter, my almost two-year-old son Jeffrey, my sister and brother-in-law, Mary Lou and Ken, and my nephew, six-month-old Kenny.

Our entire vacation had been wonderful; the weather was perfect all week. This Saturday in July was no exception. We swam and talked and laughed all day in the bright sunshine. But as we packed up our belongings from our place by the pool, I blinked and squinted.

"Chlorine! I guess I should have paid more attention to how much time I spent in the pool today," I confided to Walter. Past experience had taught me that for the next few days my eyes would sting and feel very irritated; my vision would be blurry.

We showered and dressed for dinner. Dad, always one to speak about his feelings openly, thanked us for the wonderful time: "I am so proud to be your dad, and I'm very grateful that we spent this week together. I know I had such a great time."

After dinner, we stopped at the city's convention center, where bands were playing and people were singing and dancing. Dad picked Jeffrey up from his stroller and danced a couple of steps with him, one of his favorite things to do. He didn't finish the dance, but instead, he quietly put Jeffrey back in the stroller and sat on the bench right next to him.

"Dad, are you okay?"

"Oh, yeah, I'm okay. I guess I'm just a little tired. It's been a busy day, a busy week." He winked at me and smiled. "Don't look so worried. I'm fine, just fine." That, too, was typical of Dad, never wanting to bring attention to himself, never wanting anyone to worry about him.

"Just the same, please promise me you'll see the doctor on Monday."

He looked at me and hesitated before speaking. I thought he'd be annoyed because he never liked to go to the doctor, and never liked reminders about going, either. Instead, he smiled faintly and said, "All right. You win. I promise I'll go."

I smiled my approval. "You'd better go! Or I'll keep at you until you do!" I teased, not wanting him to know fully the extent of my concern.

"I think I'll head back to the room now," Dad said quietly after listening to the band for a few more minutes. We were surprised because this was Dad's favorite thing to do on vacation: go to the town's band concert, listen to the music, and dance with Jeffrey in his arms.

"Maybe we should all go back to the hotel now," suggested Mom, as she began to gather their belongings.

"Maybe with a little rest, we can go to Atlantic City," agreed Dad. Going to Atlantic City had been a possible destination for our last night of vacation, since it was close to where we were staying.

We returned to our rooms. I waited a while, and went to my parents' room. Dad was sitting on the edge of the bed, encouraging my mother to go to Atlantic City. "I think you should go. I'm a little tired now, but you should go. You'll enjoy it."

Before long, plans were in place: Mary Lou, Walter, and Mom would go to Atlantic City. Ken stayed with little Kenny. I begged off because my eyes were stinging and my vision was blurry. Besides, I thought to myself, "I can stay and watch Dad."

After they left, I waited for just a few minutes, and went to check on Dad. He was sitting in a chair by the door. He was leaning forward, looking down at the floor. That was not like Dad, usually a robust and jovial man.

"Dad, are you okay?" It was hard to hide my concern this time, but I did the best I could.

He looked up at me, gave me a weak smile, and replied, "Just feeling a little upset, that's all. Maybe I had too good a dinner." He smiled his weak smile at me again.

"Dad, I'll be right back." I knew I had to get help, but I didn't want to upset him. I leaned over to kiss him, and I touched his arm; it was cold and clammy. I ran to the front desk and told the young man on duty that I thought my father was in some trouble. I described the symptoms, and about touching his arm, and the clamminess of his skin. He said he was a member of the city's rescue squad. "I'll be right down to the room," he promised.

I ran to check on Jeffrey. He was sleeping peacefully so I ran back down the hall to Dad's room. "What am I going to tell him?" I worried to myself. "He's going to be upset that I caused a ruckus for no reason."

I knocked lightly on the door, and went in. Dad was now sitting on the edge of the bed. "Dad, I told the man at the front desk about you. He's on the rescue squad and he's coming here to see you."

Instead of, "Why did you go and do that?" which I expected to hear, I heard, "Okay, thanks." That made me even more nervous. Dad was ill; I knew it, he knew it. We just didn't know how ill at the time. That would become apparent in the next few hours and the days to come.

Before long, the rescue squad arrived, coinciding with my family's return from Atlantic City. They returned almost immediately upon arriving there. Walter did not have a tie, so he was not allowed inside the casino. They took that as a sign that they should come back, which they did, only to find that they had made the correct decision. They came into the hotel room only minutes after the ambulance had arrived.

"Donna! What—?" was all anyone could manage to say. I quickly told them. One of the EMTs approached us. "Your dad is having a heart attack and needs to be hospitalized. The hospital is about a half hour away. Follow us!"

We quickly made plans for Ken to stay with both Kenny and Jeffrey, and followed the man to the ambulance. The ride to the hospital seemed interminable. The silence was broken with whispered words of prayer lifted to the Lord.

The prayers and silence continued as we waited for the doctor to speak to us after evaluating Dad. The doctor walked into the room, looking grim. "Your husband has suffered a major heart attack," he told my mother. "There appears to be a blockage in the aorta. There has been major damage to the heart muscle."

"What can we do to help him?" we asked, hoping beyond hope that the small community hospital would have some resources that would restore Dad's health.

"We've done what we can for him here," the doctor stated in a very matter-of-fact manner. Then, in answer to the pleading looks on our faces, he said "But I just ended an internship at a specialized heart and lung center. It's about an hour away from here. I can call and see if we can get him evaluated for further treatment there."

More prayers were whispered. Shortly afterward,

Dr. Weiner returned, smiling. "It's all set. The ambulance will take your husband tomorrow morning. Once you get there, you'll have to fill out the admission papers," he instructed my mother.

We all breathed a sigh of relief. What a wondrous thing, a doctor at this hospital has connections to a hospital renowned for helping people with heart problems. We weren't past all of our problems, but with this, we overcame a major hurdle. Maybe they could help Dad. We were determined to find out.

After Dad was safely in the capable hands of the cardiologists and nurses at the heart hospital, I had some time to reflect on the past few days. It never occurred to me until then that at some point while I was checking on Dad, my eyes stopped hurting. I clearly saw the miracles formed by the hand of God in the twists and turns of these life-changing events. How else to explain my temporary eye irritation that kept me near my father and then left as quickly as it had come, the young EMT who happened to be on duty at the front desk that night, culminating with the trip to the small community hospital that had as its Emergency Room doctor someone with connections to a specialized hospital that suited our desperate needs?

These may not be what some think of as "major"

miracles but, on the other hand, I don't know if any miracle can be classified as "small." However, I am very sure that this series of miracles came together to answer my family's prayers that night and the days that followed. We were given the gift of having Dad for an additional ten months, and we will always be grateful for the extra time that we had to spend with him.

I am also convinced that on that day, and every other day, there is Someone watching over us.

I Saw the Hand of God Move

by Joe Stevenson

————— ‧※‧ —————

I've always believed in God. But over the years my beliefs about who God is—and what He can do—have changed. It wasn't until my son was gravely ill that I learned you can believe in God and yet not know Him at all.

Know. Knowledge. Logic. When I was younger, those were the words I wanted to live by. As a child I contracted scarlet fever, and this illness ruled out my ever playing sports or roughhousing around. The only real adventures I could go on were adventures of the mind. I read books with a vengeance—*Great Books of the Western World*, and the volumes of Will and Ariel Durant, and literally thousands more—and out of my reading I formed my strongest beliefs. I believed in logic; in the mind's ability to put all creation into neat, rational categories.

At the same time I was growing up in a strongly Christian family, and so I believed in God. But I insisted—and my insistence caused a lot of arguments—that God Himself was also a Being bound by logic and His own natural laws. I guess I pictured God as a great scientist. Miracles? No, God couldn't and wouldn't break laws in that way. When my family told me that Christianity means faith in a loving, miraculous God, I turned away and went looking for other religions—ones that respected the rational mind above all.

As I became a man, my belief in rationality helped me in my career. I became a salesman for the Bell System, and when I needed to formulate sales strategies and targets, logic unlocked a lot of doors on the way to success.

But other doors seemed to be closed. I felt dry, spiritually empty, and anxious. I tried meditation, ESP, and so on, but the emptiness increased to despair.

In utter defeat, I turned to God in prayer. His Spirit answered with, "I don't simply want belief that I exist. I want you, your will, your life, your dreams, your goals, your very being. And I want your faith,

faith that I am sufficient for all your needs." My despair overcame my logic and I yielded all to Him. But just saying you have faith is not the same as having it. In my mind, I still had God in a box.

Maybe that's why I never thought to pray when my oldest son Frank came home from first grade one day and said he didn't feel well. What would God care about stomach flu? A doctor whom my wife Janice and I had consulted wasn't very alarmed about Frank's illness at first. "It's really not too serious," the doctor assured us, "just a bad case of the flu complicated by a little acidosis. Give him this medicine and in a few days he'll be fine."

But Frank wasn't fine, not at all. The medicine worked for a day or so, but then his symptoms—the gagging, choking and vomiting—came back more violently. His small, six-year-old frame was bathed in sweat and racked with convulsions. We checked him into the local hospital for further testing, but later in the evening our doctor said the original diagnosis was correct. "He's just got a real bad case of it," we were told.

I went to work the next day fully expecting to take Frank and Janice home that night, but when I stopped at the hospital to pick them up, our doctor was there to meet me. "I'd like to have a word with you two," he said, showing Janice and me into a private room.

"A problem, Doctor?" I asked.

"Further testing has shown our previous diagnosis was incorrect. We think your son has acute nephritis. It's a serious kidney disease...." He paused, and I could feel the blood running from my face. "But we've found that in children there's a good chance of a full recovery. Your son has a ninety percent chance of being as good as new."

But by ten o'clock the next morning, the news was worse. Sometime during the night, Frank's kidneys had failed. Janice and I rushed to the hospital again.

"X-rays show Frank's kidneys are so badly infected that no fluid will pass through them," we were told. "The odds aren't in his favor anymore. If those kidneys don't start working within forty-eight hours, I'm afraid your son will die."

I looked at Janice, watching the tears well in her eyes as a huge lump formed in my throat. I took her hand in mine, and slowly we walked back to Frank's room. We were too shocked, too upset to even talk. All afternoon we sat at Frank's bedside, watching, stroking his matted blond hair, wiping his damp forehead. The stillness of the room was broken only by the beeps and blips of the machines monitoring little Frank's condition. Specialists would occasionally come, adjust a few tubes, make some marks on Frank's chart, and then silently go. I searched their eyes for an answer, for some glimmer of hope, and got nothing. When our minister came to pray for our son, I could only cry in desperation.

Late that evening, after Frank was asleep, we went home. Friends were waiting with a hot meal, words of encouragement, and news of a vast prayer chain they had begun. And for a fleeting moment, I thought I saw in Janice's eyes the spark of hope that I had been looking for from the doctors all afternoon.

By the following morning, that spark of hope had ignited a flame of confidence in Janice. "I turned Frank's life over to God last night," she told me excitedly, before we were even out of bed. "I feel a real peace about what's going to happen, that God's will is going to be done."

"God's will?" I said angrily. "What kind of God makes little boys get sick? He doesn't care!" And I rolled over. Peace? God's will? No, little Frank would need more than that to get well.

But my anger didn't stop me from trying to reason with God. All that morning, while Janice kept a hospital vigil, I begged and pleaded and screamed at

God, daring Him to disprove my skepticism, trying to goad Him into action.

"Who do You think You are?" I shouted once. "Why are You doing this to my son? He's only six! Everybody says You're such a loving God—why don't You show it?" I yelled until I was exhausted. Finally, convinced my arguments were falling on deaf ears, I took our other children to a neighbor and headed to the hospital, thinking this might be the last time I'd see my son alive.

I never arrived; at least, a part of me didn't. In the car on the way, this Higher Being, this remote Power, this unjust God, spoke to me through His Spirit. I felt His presence, soothing my still-hot anger. And I heard His voice, gentle, reassuring. He reminded me that I had made a commitment to Him, that I had promised to trust Him with my life, my all. And He had promised to take care of me, in all circumstances. *"Take Me out of the box you've put Me in,"* He said, *"and let Me work."* By the time I parked the car, my heart was beating wildly. I sat for a few moments longer and uttered but two words in reply to all that had happened: "Forgive me."

By the time I reached Frank's room, I knew what I needed to do as clearly as if someone had given me written instructions. There had been no change in

Frank's condition, so I sent Janice home to get some rest. Then I walked over to Frank's bed. Placing shaking hands on where I thought his kidneys should be, I prayed as I never believed I would ever pray. "God, forgive me for my ego, for trying to make You what I want You to be. If You will, heal my son; and if You won't, that's all right, too. I'll trust You. But, please, do either right now, I pray in Christ's name. Amen."

That was all. There were no lightning flashes, no glows, no surges of emotion like the rushing wind, only the *blip-blip-blip* of monitors. I calmly sat down in a chair, picked up a magazine, and began to wait for God's answer. There was only one difference. For the first time in my life, I knew I was going to get one.

Within moments my eyes were drawn from the magazine to a catheter tube leading from Frank's frail-looking body. That tube was supposed to drain fluid from his kidneys, but for nearly two days it had been perfectly dry, meaning Frank's kidneys weren't working at all. But when I looked closely at the top of the tube, I saw a small drop of clear fluid forming. Ever so slowly it expanded, like a drop of water forming on the head of a leaky faucet, until it became heavy enough to run down the tube and into the collecting jar.

This was the most wonderful thing I had ever seen—the hand of God, working. I watched the tube, transfixed, fully expecting to see another drop of fluid form. In about two minutes, I did. Soon, the drops were coming regularly, about a minute apart. With every drip, I could hear God saying to me, *"I am, and I care."*

When the nurse came in on her regular half-hour rounds, she could barely contain her excitement. "Do you see this, do you see this?" she shouted, pointing to the collecting jar. "Do you know that this is more fluid than your son has excreted in the past forty-eight hours combined?" She grabbed the catheter and raised it, saying she wanted to get every drop, then rushed off.

Within minutes she was back. Grabbing a chair, she sat down next to me and, excitedly, we watched drops of fluid run down the tube. We were both awed at what was happening; for half an hour we murmured only short sentences. "Isn't God good?" she asked me once, and I nodded. When she finally got up to call the doctor, I went to call Janice.

An hour and a half later, one of the specialists assigned to Frank's case arrived. Taking one look at the collector, he told us that it was a false alarm, that the fluid was too clear. Anything coming from a kidney as infected as Frank's was would be rust-colored and filled with pus. No, he said, the fluid had to be coming from somewhere else. But I knew—Frank was well again.

By the next morning more than five hundred centimeters of the clear fluid had passed into the collector, and it continued as the doctors ran tests and X-rays to try to determine its origin.

Finally, two days later, our doctor called us into his office. "Joe, Janice, I think we've been privileged to witness an act of God. All the X-rays taken in the last two days not only show no kidney infection, they show no sign that there was ever an infection. Frank's blood pressure and blood poison levels have also dropped suddenly.... It is a definite miracle."

And this time I wasn't about to argue. At last I fully believed in a God whose love knows no bounds...not the bounds of logic, not the hold of natural laws. Faith. That's what I now had...that and the knowledge that one's belief in God is essentially hollow if the belief isn't founded on faith.

God's Property

by Joanna Daniel

The headaches and exhaustion that had plagued me for weeks were getting worse. Finally a specialist diagnosed my problem as hemolysis—the destruction of the red blood cells. The type I had was fatal—usually in a matter of months. And I was only forty-five, with a husband and three children to care for.

"Your blood cells are bursting like little balloons," doctors told me. "But we still don't know the reason. Your condition is so advanced that any treatments or drugs are just too risky. All we can do is wait."

Alone in a hospital room, I was nauseous with fear. I was especially concerned for my little daughter Marcia. She was my Down's syndrome child; how would she get along?

Marcia! Whenever she was frightened, she'd call out: "Devil, take your hands off me! I'm God's property!"

She'd heard that on television. We'd always smiled at her simple trust. Yet now I wondered: did I have enough faith to say those words—and mean them? With unusual boldness, I said, "Satan, take your hands off me! I'm God's child and I won't die till He's through with me!"

Almost immediately, the nausea left. I felt Christ's presence!

I went home, but returned to the hospital three times a week for blood tests. By the second visit, the doctor reported that my blood count had climbed three points. "What's happening?" he asked, bewildered.

Five months later—without drugs or treatment of any kind—my blood count was normal. There was no trace of the hemolysis. The doctors were astounded.

But I wasn't, and today I often take Marcia in my arms, hold her tight, and say, "Devil, get away! We're both God's property!"

Unexpected *Healing*

by Margaret Murray

One September, Uncle Wilson, my mother's only brother, underwent surgery for an intestinal tumor. The doctors, discovering a tumor too large and complex to remove, gave him from four to six months to live. Uncle Wilson was brought home to spend his remaining days. With no wife to see to his needs, his care fell to my mother, her two sisters, and us nieces and nephews.

We all worked hard to make Uncle Wilson comfortable, but he was bedridden, helpless, and in great pain. Day after day we tended to his needs, tried to soothe his fears. And every night before bed I knelt and asked God to heal this good, kind man.

Ten hard months later, Uncle Wilson took a turn for the worse. I was called and told to come at once. I stood by his bed, waiting for the rescue squad ambulance to come, and even in his pain Uncle Wilson tried to communicate his love and thanks by kissing my hand.

By now I was no longer praying for his healing, but simply asking that God take my uncle to be with Him. And then, early in the morning of his third day in the hospital, my sister and I were with him when Uncle Wilson suddenly opened his eyes, and in a loud and clear voice he cried, "My God! My God! My God!" My sister and I were wonder-struck.

Uncle Wilson died soon after, but my family was sustained by his words. My uncle, you see, had been deaf and mute since birth. These words were the first he had ever spoken.

A Note
from the Editors

Guideposts, a nonprofit organization, touches millions of lives every day through products and services that inspire, encourage, and uplift. Our magazines, books, prayer network, and outreach programs help people connect their faith-filled values to their daily lives. To learn more, visit Guideposts.org.